The Ocean's Call
A Transatlantic Passage

Ernst Rothe

The Ocean's Call: A Transatlantic Adventure
Copyright © 2021 Ernst Rothe

Produced and printed by Stillwater River Publications. All rights reserved. Written and produced in the United States of America. This book may not be reproduced or sold in any form without the expressed, written permission of the author.

Visit our website at
www.StillwaterPress.com
for more information.

First Stillwater River Publications Edition

ISBN: 978-1-955123-53-2

Library of Congress Control Number: 2021919447

1 2 3 4 5 6 7 8 9 10
Written by Ernst Rothe
Cover image by Ernst Rothe
Cover design by Lindsay Whelan
Interior book design by Matthew St. Jean
Published by Stillwater River Publications,
Pawtucket, RI, USA.

Publisher's Cataloging-In-Publication Data
(Prepared by The Donohue Group, Inc.)

Names: Rothe, Ernst, 1941- author.
Title: The ocean's call : a transatlantic passage / Ernst Rothe.
Description: First Stillwater River Publications edition. | Pawtucket, RI, USA : Stillwater River Publications, [2021] |
Identifiers: ISBN 9781955123532
Subjects: LCSH: Sailing--Atlantic Ocean--21st century. | Transatlantic voyages--21st century. | Yacht racing--Atlantic Ocean--21st century. | Newport Bermuda Race (2004)
Classification: LCC GV811 .R68 2021 | DDC 797.12409163--dc23

The views and opinions expressed in this book are solely those of the author and do not necessarily reflect the views and opinions of the publisher.

The Ocean's Call

I must venture forth on the seas again to heed the Ocean's Call,
    For it is a silent call and a mysterious call, heard by sailors all.
I must venture forth to the rigging groaning and the white sails driving,
    And the cascading bow wave rushing, with dolphins leaping and diving.

I must venture forth again to the windblown seas, foaming and thundering,
    For the lure of distant lands calls adventurers to their plundering.
I must venture forth on the teeming seas, where the blown mist of a whale's spouting
    Challenges a harpooner's courage that never yields to self-doubting.

I must venture forth again to the top of the storm-tossed mast,
    For the boundless fury calls each man to strain to his very last.
I must venture forth where each sailor has one hand for himself and one for his ship,
    And across a flooded deck he must struggle, as the rails roll and dip.

I must venture forth again to the moonlight flickering on ruffled waves,
    To the night's celestial splendor from whence a mortal sailor an answer craves.
I must venture forth, where the ocean's expanse stretches infinitely far,
    Over centuries charted by man's navigation, sighting both sun and star.

I must venture forth on the seas again to heed the Ocean's Call,
    For it streams in a sailor's blood, as currents rush past landfall.
I must venture forth where flood tides carry ships to safety at voyage's end
    To an eternal harbor, may I be lifted by a celestial tide at my final journey's end.

—Ernst Rothe, December 21, 2004

This account of the sloop *Diva's* voyage from June 18th to July 14th, 2004, from Newport, Rhode Island, to St. George, Bermuda, and then to Kinsale, Ireland, is dedicated to our wives and significant others:

Angela F.
Peggy L.
Ruth M.
Sylvia Q.
Nancy R.
Doris Z.

As members of *Diva's* crew, living together in crowded quarters for five weeks, we now admire even more their endurance and stoicism regarding *some* of our characteristics. On the other hand, the *sum* of our characters was, and still is, meritorious enough to sustain us across the perilous North Atlantic, thus rendering us deserving of their tender affections.

Contents

The Ocean's Call	*iii*
List of Illustrations	*ix*
Acknowledgements	*xi*
Introduction	*xiii*
Transatlantic Passage	1
Captain and Crew	5
S/Y *Diva*	13
Newport	19
Newport-Bermuda Race	23
Part 1 – Bermuda Race	**27**
Bermuda	73
Part 2 – Transatlantic Passage	**81**
Appendix A – Crew's CVs	*173*
Appendix B – Glossary	*183*

List of Illustrations

1.	Ocean's Call	3
2.	Transatlantic Route	3
3.	Crew Aboard *Diva* Departing Newport	5
4.	Edwin G. (Garry) Fischer, Skipper and Navigator	6
5.	A Howard Eisenberg	7
6.	Rob Leeson	8
7.	Neil Macaulay, Weather Forecaster and Tactician	9
8.	John C. Quinn	10
9.	Ernst Rothe	11
10.	Sailing Yacht (S/Y) *Diva* Departing Newport	12
11.	*Diva's* Profile	14
12.	S/Y *Diva's* Stowage Spaces	18
13.	Newport Harbor Aerial View	22
14.	*Harbor Court*, New York Yacht Club's (NYYC) Station at Newport	22
15.	The Starting Line (2004) and Newport Approaches	28
16.	Bermuda Race Start, 2004	28
17.	Nancy (AKA Mariposa) and her Hat with Ernst	32
18.	Gulf Stream Eddy	34
19.	Gulf Stream Squall	46
20.	Rothe's Gulf Stream Wind Pattern Theory	51
21.	Class-12 Positions as of 0800 June 20th	52
22.	A Useful Rig	55
23.	Class-12 Fleet Positions June 21st	58
24.	Ernst's Errant Star	61
25.	Class-12 Positions as of 0800 June 22nd	63
26.	Rothe's Theory of Ruffled Water Optics	66
27.	Approaches to Bermuda (Chart)	68
28.	Greater Bermuda (Chart)	69
29.	Point Able and Icebergs (Chart)	85
30.	Bermuda Disappears Astern	86
31.	In the Shade of *Diva's* Cockpit Awning	93

32.	Ernst at the Helm of *Palawan-2* in the North Atlantic, 1960	97
33.	Great Circle Route	102
34.	North Atlantic Squall Line	120
35.	*Wind Seeking Technique*	122
36.	*Palawan-2* Storming to Windward off Scotland's Coast, 1960	125
37.	Thomas J. Watson, Jr., on *Palawan-2's* Helm in the North Atlantic	125
38.	What I Saw off our Starboard Bow	143
39.	Collision-at-Sea Avoidance Maneuver	144
40.	Ernst's Well-Bread Loaf	153
41.	Fastnet Rock Lighthouse	170
42.	Compass Rose	185

Acknowledgements

No book is written solely by its author. My greatest gratitude is extended to my wife, Nancy, for her patient encouragement, her dedication to our shared vision, her captivating photographs, her insightful suggestions, her correcting of my French, and her unerring and indefatigable proofreading, as well as her editorial improvements. I am indebted to my uncle, Dr. Edward T. Hall, Jr., whose distinguished publishing career inspired me to follow his extraordinary example, as well as to my grandparents, Heinz Warneke and Jessie Gilroy Warneke, who taught me the unique importance of intellectual curiosity and artistic creativity.

Also, I wish to express my special appreciation to Edwin (Garry) Fischer, whose spirit of adventure and leadership made the voyage possible, for his enthusiastic assistance for this publishing project. Also to Rob Leeson, Neil Macauley, and John Quinn for their editorial counsel and encouragement.

I thank our son Alden for piloting for my aerial photographs and for composing the score for the video; our son Whit for editing my video recording, poetry, and narration; and my son Ernst, Jr., for his insightful marketing suggestions and encouragement.

Further, I wish to thank my late father, Tyge E. Rothe, who taught me the fundamental seamanship skills of understanding the relationship between a sailing vessel and the propelling forces of nature,

And to the late Mr. Thomas J. Watson, Jr., who broadened my sailing skills to include mastery of deep-water sailing. He who inspired me to explore the unknown.

Finally, I am also indebted to all my shipmates for sharing this extraordinary experience.

Introduction

I started sailing at the age of nine. Later, as a college freshman at Brown University in 1960, I had the good fortune of racing with the Chairman of IBM, Thomas J. Watson, Jr., from Newport to Bermuda and then to Marstrand, Sweden, aboard his *Palawan-2*, an exceptionally beautiful, 54-foot mahogany sloop built by Abeking & Rasmussen in Hamburg, Germany.

In 2004, I was delighted and honored when Dr. Edwin G. Fischer, known as "Garry," invited me to race aboard his 46-foot sloop *Diva* from Newport to Bermuda, and then to cruise from there to Kinsale, Ireland.

I anticipated this transatlantic voyage would allow me to examine the changes in technology that have taken place in ocean sailing over the last forty-four years and to relive the eternal truths that govern deep water sailing. Several weeks of isolation aboard a sailboat in the middle of the North Atlantic provided an extensive opportunity to reflect upon both the nature of the experience and its lessons about life.

The book has a traditional ship's log format, divided into daily chapters that portray the details of our experience in, hopefully, a vivid manner to which I have linked my reflective discourses. For readers who are less experienced in maritime matters, I include introductory explanations of key nautical concepts and a brief glossary of commonly used nautical terms in Appendix B, in the back of the book.

I give fair warning that I make many statements *tongue-in-cheek*, and that puns are a favorite of mine. I have always enjoyed their double meanings, whereby one economizes by getting *two for one*.

My account of our voyage should help moderately accomplished sailors and others to appreciate what it is like to cross the North Atlantic under sail. Our story is as much about the sailors' attitudes required for seafaring success as it is about the daily experience of such a voyage.

To avoid tempting unprepared and foolhardy adventurers to embark upon such a trip, I have included many well-founded warnings.

Based upon my fifty years of sailing, I know that *this is a venture not lightly undertaken*. Nevertheless, I hope the reader enjoys this account of our voyage and, perhaps, considers making one someday. Above all, a transatlantic passage is a spiritual voyage of self-discovery. God speed.

—Ernst Rothe, Newport, Rhode Island,
February 19, 2007

Transatlantic Passage

The attached chart (Illustration-2) presents an overview of our route, both our first leg to Bermuda and our second from there across the North Atlantic Ocean to Ireland. The distance to Bermuda is 635 nautical miles (nm.) and from there to Kinsale, Ireland is 2750 nm., for a total of 3,385 nm. A nautical mile is 6,080 feet, which equals 1.15 statute miles of 5,280 feet. A knot is one nautical mile per hour—and is *never* referred to as "knots per hour."

Based upon an estimated, average, over-the-ground speed of 5.5 knots, we should be able to arrive in Bermuda within 4.8 days and then cross the Atlantic in 20.8 days, for a total of 25.6 days, or 3.7 weeks, underway. Our over-the-ground speed is a combination of boat speed and prevailing currents' directions and speeds. On both legs of our journey, we will be carried by the Gulf Stream at an average speed of 3.0 knots in a generally northeasterly direction. Thus, on our way to Bermuda, it will push us away from our destination, which bears southeast; while crossing the Atlantic, it will boost us generally toward Ireland. On our way to Europe, we project our speed increase to average 1.5–2.0 knots, varying as we wander in and out of the Gulf Stream, depending upon its meandering path.

Our boat speed depends upon the wind direction and strength (velocity). The prevailing winds on our projected routes are southwesterly, thus heading us on the way to Bermuda and favoring us toward Kinsale. Since the wind velocity averages 8–15 knots, I estimate we should have an average boat speed of 6.5 knots on the leg to Europe under optimum conditions.

Unfortunately, both the prevailing wind directions and average velocities apply about seventy percent of the time on the way to Ireland. If we are unlucky enough to hit the other thirty percent during a substantial portion of our passage, our average speed may drop to only 4.0 knots. Thus, under especially favorable conditions we may average 8 knots over-the-ground and arrive in Kinsale in only 14.3 days, while under unfavorable conditions we will arrive in 28.6 days. The average of these figures is 21.5 days from Bermuda to Ireland, so this is probably what we can expect.

What are considered favorable sailing conditions? Favorable involves being pushed by a moderate breeze of 10–25 knots coming from the stern with moderate sea conditions and a favoring current. In contrast, unfavorable conditions consist of a wind coming against us from the bow, either very light (under 7 knots) or excessively heavy (over 20 knots), with heavy seas that impede the boat's passage and an unfavorable current. Also, one can add rain to this scenario in order to increase the crew's discomfort. (For a detailed description, see Appendix B, Points of Sail.)

Thus, in terms of distance, duration, and sea conditions, there are obvious differences between racing to Bermuda and crossing the North Atlantic. The greatest difference for the crew, however, will be one of mentality, or attitude. The first leg is a race against competing boats, during which virtually everything is sacrificed to achieve boat speed. In theory, taking measured risks is rewarded. The intermediate goals and successes at various waypoints are obvious and transitory. On the other hand, during a long ocean passage, the sea reduces life to its most elemental terms: survival and safety, combined with reasonable progress toward one's goal. These truths quickly become self-evident to anyone on the ocean.

Aside from one's vessel's seaworthiness and the adequacy of her provisions, the competency of the crew members and their ability to work together as a team are absolute requirements for survival on the ocean and a successful voyage. One's individual survival depends completely on the collective effort of all the crew. *We are all connected in an obvious yet mysterious way*, some of which we understand and some of which we cannot fathom.

1. Ocean's Call (ER)
The 72-foot sloop *Djinn* approaching the race's finish under a front of squall clouds off Bermuda in 1960, as seen from *Palawan-2*.

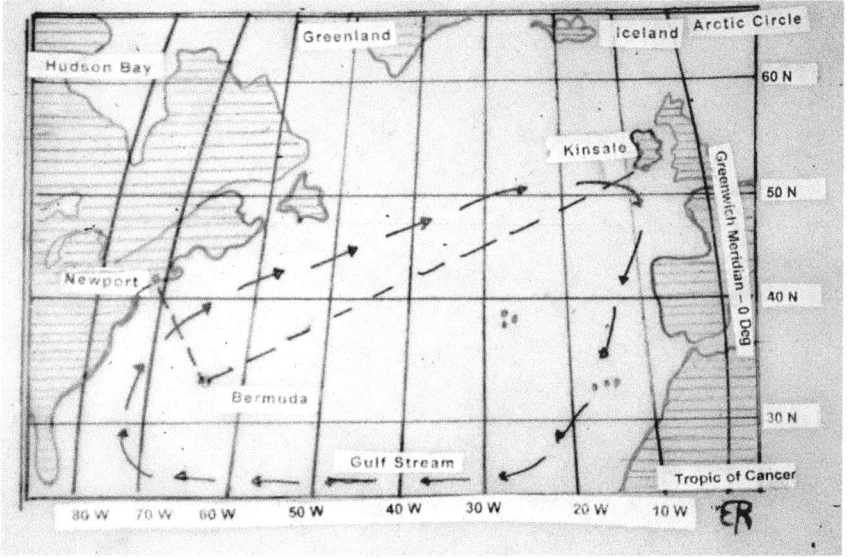

2. Transatlantic Route (ER)

Captain and Crew

3. Crew Aboard *Diva* Departing Newport (NER)
"Associate yourself with men of good quality and you esteem your own reputation; for it is better to be alone than in bad company."
—*George Washington*

4. Edwin G. (Garry) Fischer, Skipper and Navigator (ER)
Our skipper Garry's wisdom, quick wit, quiet confidence, extensive ocean sailing experience, and warm generosity make him a natural leader, greatly respected by all. Professionally, he is a neurosurgeon and serves as the NYYC fleet physician.

5. Howard Eisenberg (NER)
Howard's ironic sense of humor, willingness to help, and quiet enthusiasm make him a welcome shipmate. On the helm he holds a course with relentless, surgical precision, absolutely heedless of raging gales and the ocean's tumult.

6. Rob Leeson (NER)

Rob's sailing expertise, quiet confidence, and subtle sense of humor help sustain our morale. Accomplished at getting a boat going in virtually any wind or sea condition, Rob applies his sail-trimming and helmsman experience quietly, allowing the boat's speed to speak for itself.

7. Neil Macaulay, Weather Forecaster and Tactician (ER)
As our Resident Scotsman, Neil takes his responsibilities seriously. His tenacity, willingness to help, and sense of humor are greatly appreciated by all. His hand steadies the kicking helm, no matter how rough the seas become.

8. John C. Quinn (JCQ)
John's steadfast enthusiasm lifts everyone's spirits. From his extraordinarily broad range of racing experience, John has honed a keen sense of how to get a boat moving at its maximum speed in virtually all wind and weather conditions.

9. Ernst Rothe (NER)

To quote a fellow crew member, "Ernst's positive approach and enthusiastic attitude—coupled with his unparalleled seamanship—ensured the entire crew remained in good spirits at all times, even during three straight days of rain and miserable conditions."

10. Sailing Yacht (S/Y) *Diva* Departing Newport (NER)
This 46-foot sloop will be the home to six intrepid sailors for the next month. It comprises their entire inhabitable portion of the world and is surrounded by a hostile sea that seeks the vessel's destruction caused by the crew's carelessness.

Sailing Yacht (S/Y) *Diva*

Before we depart, it seems appropriate for me to introduce *Diva*, our sea-borne home for the next month. She is a fiberglass Morris-46 sloop designed by Chuck Paine and built by Morris Yachts in Southwest Harbor, Maine.

S/Y *Diva's* Profile

Diva is a masthead sloop with classic hull lines above the waterline, reminiscent of the designs prevailing in the 1930s through the 1950s. She has an updated semi-displacement hull below the waterline with a fairly long trapezoidal keel, whose center of resistance appears to be slightly forward of the midpoint along her waterline. A ventral skeg runs aft from the keel to a fin section to which the rudder is attached, located between the helm and the overhanging stern.

Her principal dimensions are:

Displacement:	24,500 lbs, of which 9,630 are keel ballast
Length overall:	45' – 11"
Length on waterline:	35' – 6"
Beam:	13'
Draft:	5' – 6"
Sail area:	879 ft^2
Mast height:	59'
Hull speed, upright:	7.5 knots
Fuel:	Total: 117 gal., main: 80 gal., fwd: 37 gal. (plus 40 gal. on deck for this trip)
Water:	Total 120 gal., 61 gal. port, 59 gal. starboard
Engine:	75 hp diesel (Yanmar)

Her hull is fiberglass, and the mast is aluminum with stainless steel rod rigging.

Her topsides are painted a tasteful maroon with a white boot top and a medium blue bottom. The decks are a light cream color that reduces sun glare subtly and very effectively.

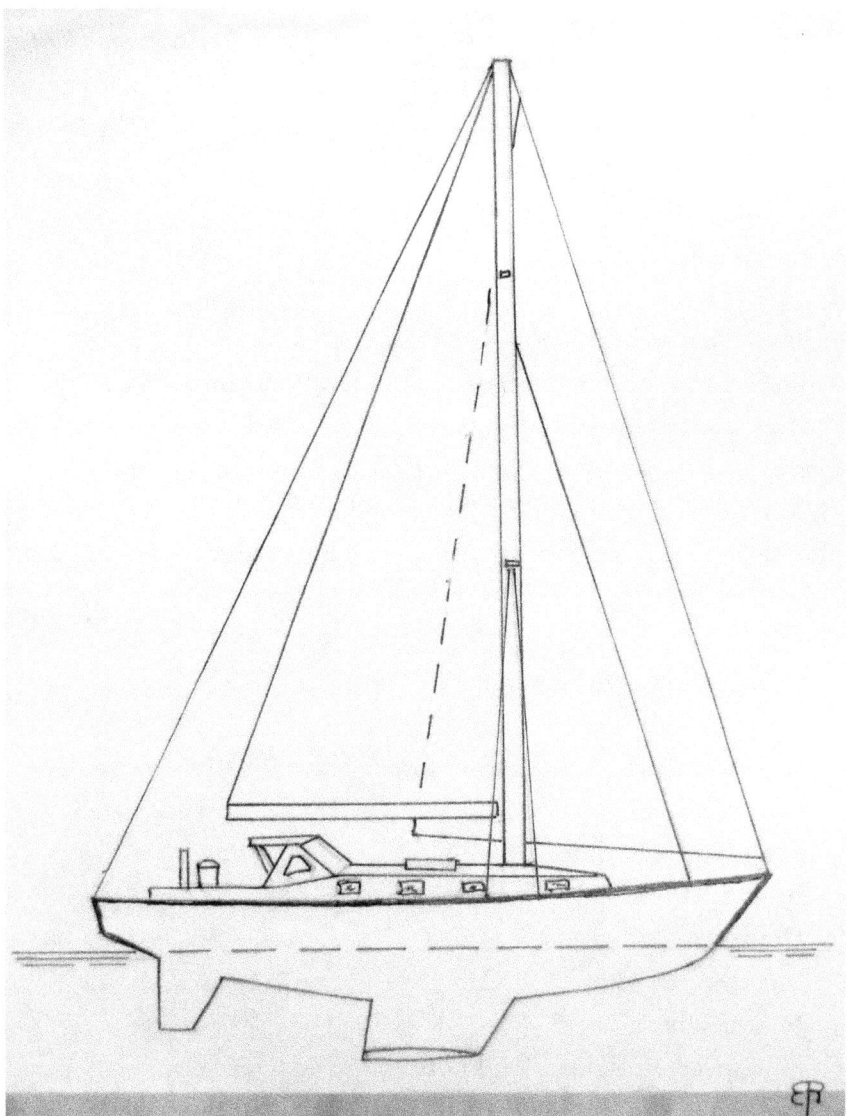

11. *Diva's* **Profile**

S/Y *Diva's* Layout

Below decks, she has antique white paneling, doors, and drawers that are framed by moldings of varnished cherry. The floorboards are of alternating strips of warm cherry and light wood. The forward bulkhead is adorned with a painting depicting the Ida Lewis Yacht Club, *Diva's* home. As a whole, the appearance is a pleasing combination of modern openness and commodious space combined with traditional elegance.

Diva's layout is a traditional and proven one, with sufficient floor area and passageway width to permit unobstructed movement below decks. It is arranged as follows, from the bow moving aft (see Illustration 12):

Forepeak
Forward cabin
Forward head, to port
Hanging locker and drawers, to starboard
Main cabin with settee and two pilot berths, with drawers underneath
Galley, to port, with freezer, refrigerator, and gas stove
Navigator's station, to starboard
After head, to starboard, with a shower and wet locker in the adjoining after compartment
Cockpit companionway amidships
After cabin, to port

In the cockpit, there is a large sail locker beneath the starboard seat and two large lazarettes in the fantail.

Diva is generously equipped with a freshwater maker, pressurized hot and cold water, two showers, a gas stove, a refrigerator, a freezer, and a forced hot air cabin heater. In short, she has all the comforts of home. Her safety equipment includes an automatically inflating life raft with a built-in cover for weather protection, Emergency Position Indicating Radio Beacons (EPIRBs), emergency survival kits, and so forth.

Diva's principal navigation and communications equipment includes a magnetic compass, speed gauge, fathometer, radar, single-sideband radio, GPS navigational system, Inmarsat-C, and an automatic pilot. There are PC connectors to receive weather map faxes and to receive and transmit emails. At the top of the mast there is a Windex, indicating relative wind direction.

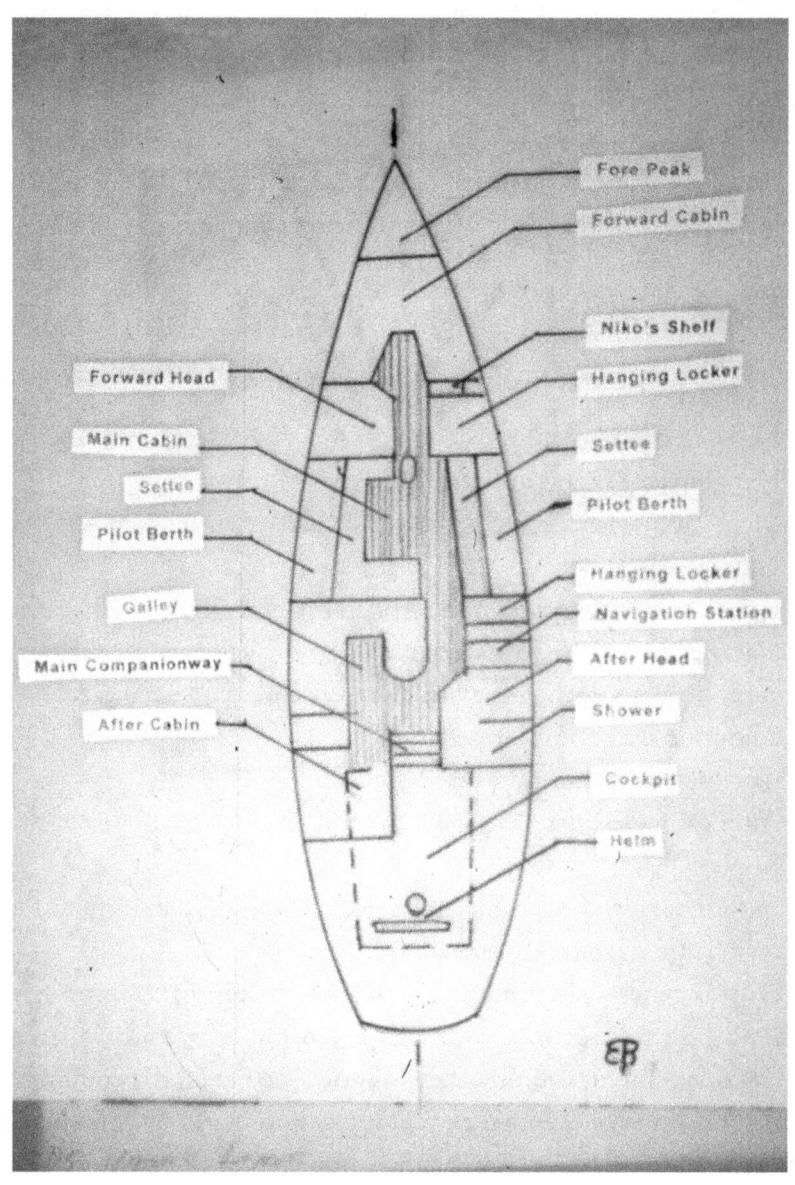

12. S/Y *Diva's* Layout (ER)

Diva's Stowage

Napoleon once observed that "an army moves on its stomach." Well, so does a navy, as does a sailing ship.

This truism raises the issue of how much food we need for this trip and where we manage to stow it. Our nourishment needs are calculated as follows:

6 days – Newport to Bermuda
19 days – Bermuda to Ireland
―――――――
25 days – subtotal
 5 days – 20 % reserve
―――――――
30 days – Total

Daily, we serve three meals per person for six people, which equals 18 meals per day. For 30 days, this totals 540 meals during the combined voyages.

How do we manage to stow all these supplies on a 46-foot sailboat? Only with a great deal of ingenuity.

Essentially, the exterior hull shape is a curvilinear form for hydrodynamic characteristics, while the interior living quarters are rectilinear. Thus, everything is stowed in the space created between these two configurations—the gaps found in the bilges, in stowage lockers, under the bunks, in the forepeak, in the anchor chain locker, behind locker drawers, and every conceivable space available. (Illustration 13)

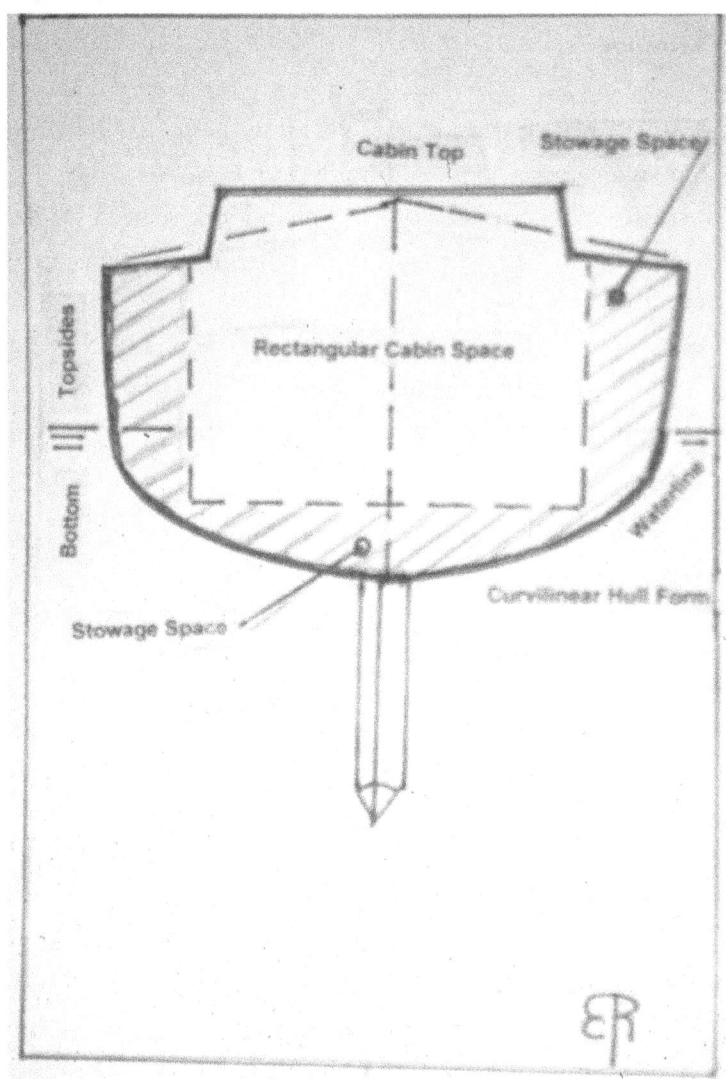

12. S/Y *Diva's* Stowage Spaces (ER)

In order to retrieve specific foods for planned meals at the appropriate time, a list and locator plan is developed in a spreadsheet format. All food supplies are wrapped in plastic bags and labeled with a waterproof felt tip pen to preserve their contents' identities. I cannot imagine any search more fruitless than looking for two cans of peas amongst seventy or eighty cans without their labels. Under such circumstances, would we have to settle for a dinner dish of onions and pineapple slices? How would that affect our stomach-sensitive morale?

Newport—America's Yachting Capital

Our race to Bermuda begins in Newport, Rhode Island. Founded in 1639, Newport is one of the oldest cities in the United States. Located on the southwestern tip of Aquidneck Island, it shares many characteristics with New York City. The island is virtually the same size as Manhattan, its harbor is a sheltered deep-water port, and its location adjacent to the Gulf Stream renders it ice-free for commerce throughout the winter, in contrast with more northerly New England ports, such as Boston.

Until the American Revolution, Newport ranked among the most prosperous seaports along the East Coast, rivaling Philadelphia and outshining New York City. Many elegant merchant houses graced Newport's waterfront, which was lined with bustling wharves, warehouses and shipyards to serve their maritime fleets. Almost for the duration of the Revolution, Newport was occupied by British troops who demolished many local homes for use as firewood, thereby effectively razing the town. During this extended period of extreme adversity, many residents fled and resettled elsewhere permanently. After the Revolution, New York ascended to challenge Philadelphia as the primary East Coast port, and Newport receded into history, never to rise again as a merchant port.

In the early to mid-1800s, members of the Southern aristocracy discovered Newport's salubrious seaside climate and began migrating north aboard coastal steamers every summer to escape the enervating heat of Georgia and the Carolinas. To satisfy the burgeoning demand for a seaside resort, large hotels were built in the center of town and connected to the beaches by horse-drawn trolley cars.

At the outbreak of the Civil War, the US Navy transferred its academy to the frigate *USS Constitution,* moored alongside a pier at Fort Adams, and then to a large hotel on Bellevue Avenue, near Touro Park in the center of town. After hostilities ceased, the Naval Academy returned to Annapolis, but the Navy remained ensconced. Since that time, the US Navy has committed itself to a significant presence in Newport, presently embodied by its War College.

After the Civil War, during the Gilded Age, Newport was discovered by the newly established industrial millionaires who built private palaces, known as *summer cottages,* as proof of their limitless wealth. They arrived for the summer, bringing servants and entire households in their private railcars conveyed along their own railroad company's tracks.

Generally, millionaires prefer possessions which are unattainable by common people of ordinary means (if not by you, then certainly by me), and yachts fill this requirement better than virtually anything else. Also, their large yachts need deep harbors, such as Newport's. Rare fortune combined these demands with the local availability of a brilliant naval architect known as the Wizard of Bristol. Nathaniel Herreshoff was an extraordinarily talented designer and builder, and the sailing yachts from his shipyard in Bristol, Rhode Island, became synonymous with racing victory at sea. From 1893 to 1920, Herreshoff built six America's Cup defenders. In this manner, Newport became America's Yachting Capital, and it retains this status to this day.

From 1870 until 1887, the America's Cup races were held inside New York Harbor. They moved outside Sandy Hook from 1893 through 1920, and finally relocated to the Rhode Island Sound off Newport in 1930. The races had been squeezed out of New York Harbor by nautical traffic jams. The new competitors off Newport were the fastest and second-largest racing yachts in history. Designed according to Universal Rule Measurements, they were known as J-boats. They were gigantic, with masts as high as fourteen-story buildings and capable of speeds approaching twenty knots. They campaigned in local waters until the outbreak of World War II in 1937. After WWII, their future was terminated by the increase in income taxes.

In the early 1950s, the America's Cup competition was revived when the New York Yacht Club accepted the famed International 12-Meter design as its official class. The magnitude of this change can be appreciated by comparing the two classes (measurements are in feet unless otherwise noted):

	J-Boat	**12-Meter**
Length (LOA)	135	64
Waterline (LWL)	87	45
Beam	21	12
Draft	15	9
Sail area (ft^2)	7,950	1,770
Displacement (tons)	185	28.5

In the broadest measurement terms of displacement, a 12-Meter is about one-seventh (15.5 percent) of the size of a J-Boat.

The America's Cup series resumed off Newport until 1983, when the famous trophy was captured for the first time by a challenger, *Australia-2*. Yachting's most honored trophy has not returned to Newport since then, but it seems that everyone else has.

At the time, many predicted that Newport would wither as a yachting center. Today, Newport Harbor is filled with yachting activity. It has such a demand for moorings that owners of new yachts frequently buy old, local ones merely to acquire the mooring—in many cases, they then just dump the boat formerly attached to it.

Thus, Newport became the country's yachting capital in the late 1800s and continues to play a vanguard role in this field today. The New York Yacht Club maintains its summer station here at the elegant harborside chateau *Harbor Court*, (Illustration 15) an estate previously owned by the renowned yachtsman and former NYYC Commodore, John Nicholas Brown, who campaigned his famous yacht, the 72-foot yawl *Bolero,* to many victories during several decades, starting in the 1950s.

Aside from its yachting history, why does Newport continue to play such a central role in US East Coast yachting circles? In my personal estimation, there are three principal factors. Firstly, location: Newport is situated at a convenient midpoint for boats going "down East" to summer in Maine and returning to winter in the Caribbean. The harbor entrance is located conveniently close to the Cape Cod Canal in Buzzards Bay, through which a large portion of the coastal traffic passes. Secondly, size: the harbor is large, deep, and sheltered, enabling it to accommodate large numbers of visiting yachts. Thirdly, range of services: its facilities, infrastructure, and circle of contacts make it a natural meeting site of unsurpassed efficiency for anyone involved in yachting activities.

13. Newport Harbor Aerial View (AAR)

14. *Harbor Court*, New York Yacht Club's (NYYC) Station at Newport (ER)

The NYYC launch, *Navette,* is named after J.P. Morgan's express steam launch that ferried him from Wall Street to his estate outside New York City in Long Island.

The Newport–Bermuda Race (NBR): Yachting History

Second only to the America's Cup races, this regatta is generally regarded as one of the sailing world's most prestigious, ranking with such events as Great Britain's Fastnet Race and Australia's Sydney-Hobart Race. Since the NBR is open to anyone with a seaworthy sailing yacht and sufficient financial resources, it has become very popular amongst east coast US yachtsmen. Because of its prestige, it is often over-subscribed, and many qualified sailors' applications are rejected.

From a sailor's point of view, the NBR's distance of 635 nautical miles renders it a unique opportunity to experience true blue-water sailing for a reasonably convenient time period, since the offshore passage averages four to five days for most boats. In addition, the destination is a uniquely attractive experience. Bermuda is a singularly romantic tropical island with a sophisticated heritage from the legendary British Empire. Mark Twain once described it as "an earthbound heaven." Honestly, who *wouldn't* want to visit there?

Held on even years, the Newport–Bermuda Race is the oldest recurring ocean race in the world. As surprising as it may seem, the first race started from Graves End Bay located on the eastern side of New York Harbor in 1906. The rhumb line (magnetic) course (see p. 45) was 150 degrees, and the first boat finished in 89 hours, or 3.7 days, at an average speed of seven knots.

According to the Race Committee's subsequent studies of the prevailing wind patterns, 25 percent of the winds are from the southwest and 15 percent from the west. From this, they concluded the NBR's racing conditions were too easy. In order to increase the race's competitiveness, they moved the starting line further northeast, forcing boats to sail closer to the wind and thereby introducing greater uncertainty concerning the outcome.

To accomplish this, in 1908, they moved the starting line to Marblehead, Massachusetts, with a rhumb line course of 172 degrees. Their sophisticated, anticipatory calculations were demolished by a rogue storm's strong easterly winds. Having learned about the reliability of prevailing conditions, the Race Committee returned the start to New York City's harbor.

In the years immediately following World War I, the Race Committee decided to move the Bermuda Race's start to New London, Connecticut, located near the eastern exit of the Long Island Sound into the Atlantic. During that era, New London's popularity was increased by the Yale-Harvard crew races held there on the Thames River in June, while the popularity of New York Harbor was decreased by the upsurge in commercial traffic. Five Bermuda races started in New London, until it was deemed too provincial for some yachtsmen's tastes. In 1932, the race's start was moved to Montauk Point on the eastern end of Long Island. This arrangement lasted only one season, terminating with the race's transfer back to New London in 1934.

Finally, in 1936, the Bermuda Race Committee moved the starting line to Newport, Rhode Island, thereby pleasing so many parties and participants that it has become a fixture in the yacht racing world.

This year's NBR fleet consists of one hundred and sixty entries, divided into thirteen classes of similarly sized boats. In order to equalize a yacht's opportunity to win, each is assigned a handicap time allowance based upon the length of the race. Using the Americap rating system, this is calculated by using a boat's measurements to determine its theoretical speed and, from that, its projected finishing time. As a result, the larger, faster boats *give time* to the smaller, slower ones. Race prizes, usually impressive silver trophies, are awarded for overall fleet performance and for placement within one's class.

The absolute requirement for entering the race is that a vessel be constructed and equipped in a properly seaworthy manner. Before departure, every boat is thoroughly inspected by a certified official of the hosting organization, the Cruising Club of America (CCA).

Presently, the minimum required boat length is 40 feet, and the maximum permitted length is 85 feet. Depending upon the winds, a 40-footer can expect to sail the course at an average speed of 5.5 knots for an elapsed time of 115 hours, or 4.8 days. Under very favorable conditions, a maxi speed machine may average 15 knots for a time of 42 hours, or 1.8 days.

The 2004 "Newport–Bermuda Race" Sponsors were the Cruising Club of America (CCA) and the Royal Bermuda Yacht Club (RBYC), with local hosting in Newport provided by the New York Yacht Club (NYYC).

PART I

Newport–Bermuda Race

Newport, Rhode Island
to
St. George, Bermuda

June 18th to June 23rd, 2004

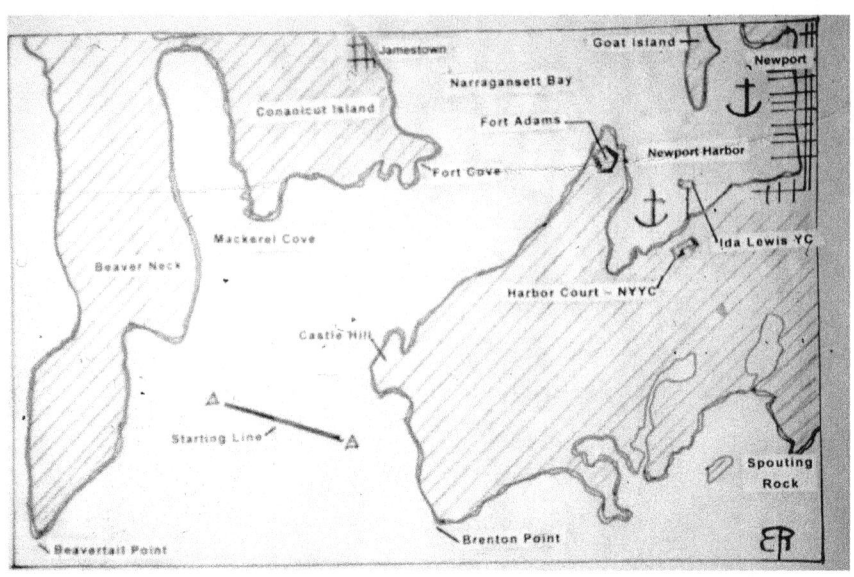

15. The Starting Line (2004) and Newport Approaches (ER)

16. Bermuda Race Start, 2004 (NER)
The start of Class-10 maxi boats, capable of speeds in excess of 20 knots. With a length of 85 feet, each yacht costs $10 million to build and $5 million annually to operate.

Friday, 18 June 2004 – Newport – 1st Day

Our long-awaited day of departure arrives, and we make our final preparations for the start of the Newport–Bermuda Race. It seems a long time ago, many months, that Garry asked me to join his crew to cross the Atlantic. Our preparation must be thorough, comprehensive, and accurate to anticipate every need and every contingency. Once we have shoved off and are out in the middle of the ocean, any deficiency cannot be rectified—only its consequences suffered.

Thus, months in advance we imagined the various shipboard scenarios that we might face and sought the advice of friends who have made the voyage before us, as well as scanned weather data for prevailing conditions. All of us made lists of our personal needs, mostly of sufficient quantities of clothing for various weather conditions. We wanted to bring great quantities, yet we could not bring too much; our personal stowage space would be limited to three small drawers, plus our share of the hanging locker. Aside from insuring our own comfort, we wished to avoid causing discomfort for other crew members—for example, by not wearing wet, dirty, smelly socks around the confines of the cabin.

My own sailing gear and stowage considerations are complicated by the fact that I plan to tour Ireland and southwestern Scotland for two weeks following our arrival in Kinsale. Thus, I must bring sufficient shore clothing, as well.

Our captain, with the assistance of his crew, has prepared *Diva* for the voyage by testing the emergency survival gear, identifying important replacement parts for key equipment, planning the navigation methodology, testing the instrumentation, calculating the amount of consumable supplies required and planning their stowage (as well as their location procedure), and calculating the fuel requirements. This phase of the plan was carried out during the four weeks prior to our departure.

If we are not fully ready now, it is too late for regrets. I am haunted by the thought that I may have forgotten something important.

0800 – In the Rothe household, our elder son Alden, 25 years old, wakes us up early with a distress call from a parking lot in Florida, where he has just incurred a minor scrape with his automobile. To resolve legal matters, we fax documentation immediately to the local police department. As if we did not have enough excitement this morning. Why do emergencies always happen at the least convenient moment?

Alden is en route to take the Air Force Officers' entrance examination. I hope that he will be able to steady his nerves and score well.

My wife, Nancy, then drives me down to NYYC's Newport Station, *Harbor Court*.

Nancy is an accomplished sailor in her own right—a real expert in sail handling, trimming, and steering, with a sharpened sense of how to maximize a boat's speed. Once, as a teenager, she was sailing at her summer camp on Lake Champlain when the rudder fell off. Undaunted, she steered her boat by varying the trim of her sails and successfully navigated her disabled craft back to the anchorage. Upon arrival, she expertly maneuvered the boat into the wind and caught her mooring. Every experienced sailor readily recognizes the excellence of this accomplishment.

I wish that she were accompanying us, but her serious interest in the Newport Music Festival will keep her here.

0940 – Nancy and I take the NYYC launch *Navette* and go aboard *Diva*. Garry's tender *Presto* is tied alongside, and everyone else is already on board. Nancy stays for twenty minutes and then departs, after gently declining Garry's offer to take her with us across the Atlantic.

As Nancy leaves *Harbor Court*, I can see her in the distance driving slowly along the seawall. We wave back and forth to each other. I miss her already!

We busily stow the last of our personal gear, fill out Bermuda Customs & Immigration forms, enter Global Positioning System (GPS) navigational waypoints, and so forth. We all sense a strong undercurrent of nervous anticipation, and everyone withdraws to quiet introspection and distracting preparation. Not much talk, now.

We review the scratch sheet, the entry listing, and find that this year's fleet consists of 160 boats, divided into 13 classes. Our class is number 12, the Cruising Canvas Division, which does not allow spinnakers—those monstrous, billowing clouds of sail that, under unfavorable circumstances, overpower both the boat and the crew, wreaking vast amounts of damage and injury. Frankly, I do not miss having a spinnaker. They may be beautiful by day, but at night in a piping wind, they are howling devils that have escaped from a sail bag.

1100 – The morning is quite foggy with an estimated visibility of one to two miles. The temperature is 72 degrees F, wind is NNW (335 deg.) and dropping from ten to five knots. Gradually the fog clears, revealing the graceful Newport Bridge.

1300 – We drop our mooring and get underway, powering out of the anchorage. We are maneuvering frequently to avoid boats that are anchored closely to one another. The harbor waters are calm, but anticipating the oily, rolling swell of the Atlantic Ocean, I take two precautionary seasick pills. My sensitivity to motion makes life *hell on the high seas* for me.

1315 – Unexpectedly, *Diva's* tender, *Presto,* speeds into view with Nancy and Whit, our younger, college-age son on board. I am very, very happy to see them both. It means the world to me. With Garry's son, Teddy, at the helm, *Presto* escorts us out of the harbor.

Nancy looks inspiringly, yet casually elegant dressed in a yellow pantsuit with a large floppy straw hat bedecked with flowers. This is highly recommended in Newport, AKA "Snootport," as *just* the thing to wear for seeing off transatlantic-bound yachtsmen. (Illustration 17)

I am very relieved as Nancy tells me that Alden's problem has been solved and that he has taken his Air Force entrance exam. Well done. I can now depart with one fewer concern.

As we proceed under power past Fort Adams at the harbor entrance, we plan our start. To the uninitiated, sailboat racing starts seem a chaotic, dangerous running of the bulls. Yachts rush about in diverse directions at full speed until, at the sound of a cannon's discharge on the committee boat, they suddenly line up and dash, madly in unison, across an imaginary line in the water. All the while, the crews are shouting preemptively at each other: *Starboard tack, Hold your course, Head up, Overlap, Right of way, Buoy room, Protest,* and so forth.

17. Nancy (AKA Mariposa) and her Hat with Ernst (Anonymous)
Mariposa, with her large, floppy straw hat bedecked with flowers. *Just the thing* to wear for seeing off transatlantic-bound yachtsmen from *Snootport*.

Well, the above impression of chaos is correct, but it can be explained. The Race Committee's objective is to start all boats of a given class simultaneously, in order to preserve the equitability of the race. A starting line usually consists of a Race Committee Boat at one end and a leeward buoy at the other, anchored at a suitable distance from the RC Boat that will allow all the sailboats to cross simultaneously without colliding with one another. Generally, the starting course is aligned in such a manner so as to force boats to sail as close to the wind as possible during the start. In other words, one starts to windward. Starting times are controlled by the committee and announced to the fleet by signal flags and a starting cannon. Any boat which crosses the line before the starting gun goes off must recross the line and restart.

From the individual contestant's point of view, the objective is to start with full speed, crossing the line at the instant the starting gun goes off and have clean air, undisturbed by any competitor's backwind, or turbulence that slows one down.

The chaotic pre-start maneuvering takes place as boats seek to establish a position that will allow them to build up to full speed as they approach the line and a location in order to cross at the correct time, as well as in a position relative to other boats that gives them a clear approach to the line, free of wind interference from others. Additionally, they prefer to approach the starting line on starboard tack because this gives them right-of-way, forcing those on port tack to stand clear. For day races, known as racing around the buoys, the start heavily influences the outcome, and consequently a great deal of ulcerous angst is associated with this phase.

Today, we will be starting to leeward because of the wind direction relative to a course heading out to sea.

1450 – Starting in Class-12 in light, variable winds, north to NNE, we reach down the starting line on port tack, directly in the face of oncoming competitors who have the right-of-way on starboard tack, and then we duck quickly under the leeward buoy to cross the line. This is a very courageous starting tactic—almost impudent—and we cross the line within three seconds of the starting gun. As opera fans say, "Brava, *Diva!*" Well done, Garry.

Immediately after the gun, our sea-bound neighborhood is crowded with boats sailing alongside one another with barely ten to twenty feet separating them. There is an obviously imminent danger of collision. Many shouts ring out, "Keep your course!" The surrounding sea is so choppy from our own waves that all of us bounce about, oblivious of the ocean's swell.

I keep my eye on a strikingly elegant *Concordia* yawl with classic varnished topsides that is close alongside us. Although she is 40-feet LOA, considerably less than our 46-feet, she is keeping up with us. I admire her classic beauty and am impressed by her speed, for this is the unmistakable sign of a well-sailed boat.

Presto witnesses our well-executed start and then reverses course, heading back toward Fort Adams to return to Newport Harbor. I am saddened as Nancy and Whit disappear, breaking my heart-strung bonds with the shore. In the growing cold and spreading dampness, I palpably sense the growing, enfolding isolation of the ocean.

1530 – We must steer clear of sharp granite ledges offshore, which are marked by a series of red buoys. Finally, we leave bell buoy 2-A to port, keeping clear of Brenton Reef. The wind has veered to SE (120 deg.) and filled in to 8–10 knots. Presently, we are steering our rhumb line course of 162 degrees on a very close port reach and footing at 7.2 knots.

As a point of explanation, a rhumb line is the straight-line distance between two points on a curved surface, such as the course of a cruise ship or an airliner from Newport to Bermuda. Since sailboats are subject to winds and currents, they very seldom sail a rhumb line course.

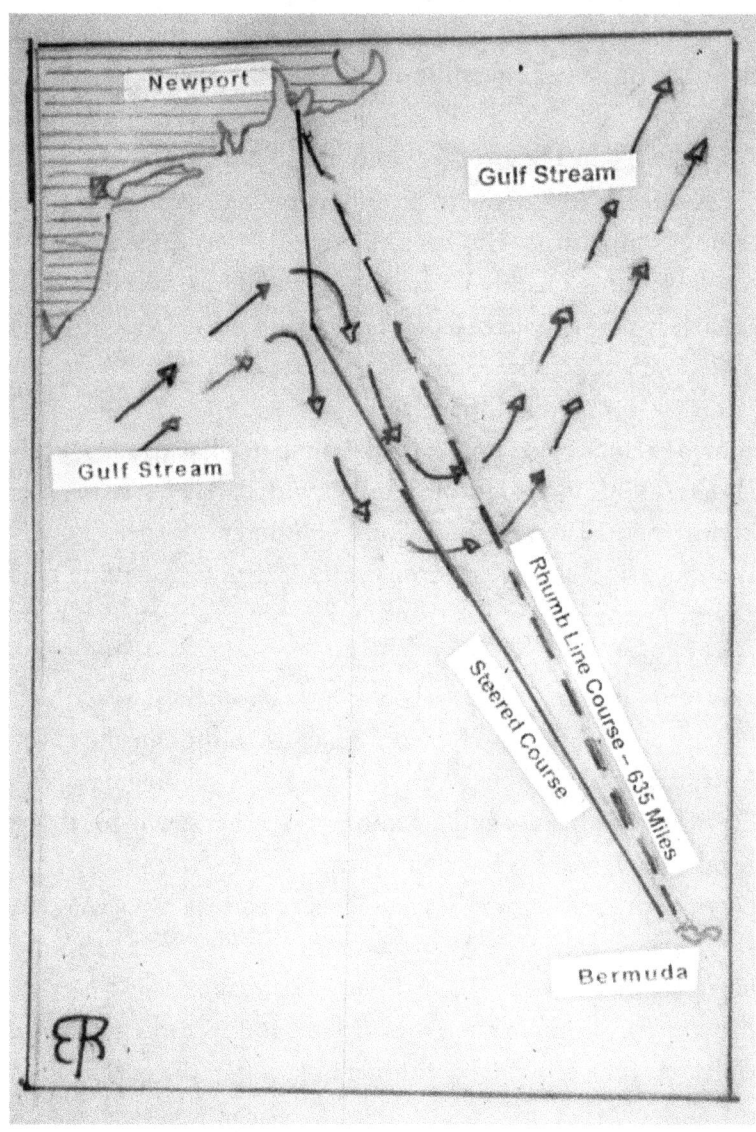

18. Gulf Stream Eddy (ER)

1830 – I enjoy a brief nap as I begin to unwind from the tension of shore-based preoccupations. Slowly, we start to focus on our short-term shipboard tasks. The wind is steady as before at 10 knots. The fog has burned off and the sun probes for gaps in the light cloud cover. Slightly chilly on deck at 69 degrees. Excellent boat speed of 7.0 knots.

A marine weather station predicts the wind will be shifting gradually from SE toward SW, and perhaps later toward W (west).

We ease our sheets (lines) slightly to steer below, or to the west, of our rhumb line course of 170 degrees. The rhumb line is a constant line of bearing, or course, toward one's destination, and not necessarily the shortest route. We have decided to try to catch the meandering Gulf Stream Eddy, a portion of the stream that doubles back on itself (Illustration 18).

Judging the correct entrance point on the Gulf Stream virtually determines the difference between winning or losing the race.

We project our course will intercept the back eddy's northerly extremity at a location that combines its reported position with our expectations of its near-term shifts. Everyone in this race is gambling on their private hunch on this matter, because the rewards for correct Gulf Stream positioning are enormous. The back eddy boosts boat speed by 3.0–3.5 knots, as opposed to a heading current of the same magnitude, for a total advantage of 6–7 knots over one's less fortunate competitors.

Diva is riding smoothly on a slight ocean swell of 2–5 feet. Rob is making our first meal underway, and the result of his competent labors in the galley is a magnificent dinner of beef and tomato soup followed by cold cooked salmon, "Hollandaze" (sic) sauce, small, boiled potatoes, and sliced pickles. Dessert is fresh fruit with freshly baked raisin oatmeal cookies. What a fabulous start. Unfortunately, no white wine is served, not even a single, small plastic cupful. When I make a suggestion to Garry that he modify the ship's abstemious policy, he reminds me that before our departure, he had offered to provide occasional spirits in return for certain health commitments. When his offer was declined by unnamed parties, Garry closed the ship's bar.

1900 – A fog rolls in, reducing the visibility to 300–500 meters, about a quarter of a mile. The wind dies temporarily. The temperature below decks is a dry 75 degrees, and temperature on deck is damp 63.5 degrees.

Generally speaking, fog is fairly prevalent along the New England coast during the summer. When the relatively warm, moisture-laden air from the heated land area is carried out over the cooler ocean by the prevailing westerly airflow, fog forms over the sea, usually a short distance offshore. Essentially, the warm, moist air condenses into a flat surface cloud—depending upon the amount of humidity in the air, its initial temperature over land, its dew point (temperature of precipitation), and the temperature of the air over the water.

Interestingly, sometimes the fog cloud is so low that the masts of ships, superstructures, and boats extend up into the clear air above the cloud, leaving the vessel itself hidden below. Thus, one can navigate safely—except for finding buoys—simply by posting a lookout topside in the rigging.

1930 – Garry announces our watch assignments. There are three watches (A, B, C) with two members each, rotating continuously. Accordingly, a typical three-day watch schedule is as follows:

Time	Hours	Day 1	Day 2	Day 3
0000				
0300	3	A	B	C
0600	3	B	C	A
1000	4	C	A	B
1400	4	A	B	C
1800	4	B	C	A
2100	3	C	A	B
2400	3	A	B	C

Thus, with a crew of six, we have two watches off duty for each one on. This is so comfortable an arrangement that we might believe that we are on a *cruise* ship instead of a *crew's* ship. Perhaps this delusion will be dispelled by the size of our ship. Well, at least it's not a *hard* ship.

2100 – Rob and I stand our first watch and everyone else is free to retire below decks. We are sailing *Diva* alone for the next three hours, responsible for her welfare and our collective safety. Variable winds ENE (60 deg.) at 5–10 knots. Our course is 160 degrees, then 165 degrees, and our boat speed varies with the wind's strength, from 4.5 to 7.5 knots.

As the evening settles in and the air temperature drops, sudden patches of very dense fog roll in. Our masthead light looms alarmingly bright, pulsating like the haunting specter of a visiting ghost.

Suddenly, we spot the lights of an unidentified sloop working its way up from astern under our lee quarter and then slipping past us to windward. This wake-up call tells us we are not sailing *Diva* as fast as we should. Rob and I respond by heightening our attention to the helm and the sail trim, and shortly thereafter we manage to pass her. The mystery sloop's crew is surprised by our rapid retaliation and shines spotlights nervously about their sails. When the fog lifts briefly, we spot two additional boats close by to windward. Racing sharpens our sailing skills even when we cannot see our competition.

Diva rolls nervously on two conflicting swells, one from the SE and the other from the SW, making steering a steady course somewhat difficult. I have been taking seasick pills regularly. I hope that they do not kill brain cells. I have so few of them. None to spare.

Seasickness. How I love sailing, and how I hate seasickness. Without doubt, it is the most useless disease in the world. In response to a vessel's motion, I empty my stomach. Now, how intelligent is that? Was this affliction devised because nature responds to a sailor's intestinal agony by calming the waves on the ocean? So far, I have never seen that happen. Seasickness simply makes a sailor's life an unbearable, relentless hell and tempts him/her to question the intelligence of the being that invented it.

For thousands of years, almost every conceivable medicinal remedy and behavioral technique has been tried in order to thwart it, so far without notable success. Fortunately, nature provides its own solution, whereby my inner ear gradually learns that the unfamiliar gyrations of my world are a natural condition to which I must adapt myself. This blessed change is known as "getting one's sea legs." I require about 36 to 48 hours to acquire mine.

I am wearing shorts, a sports shirt, a medium sweater, and a foul weather gear (FWG) top, a waterproof jacket (see page 173) to protect me against becoming soaked by the dampness of the fog. In spite of this protection, I am occasionally chilled by the wet wind.

2400 – I retire below to my bunk in the forward cabin that I share with Garry, who occupies the other bunk. Garry is a very accomplished musician who plays the violin. I soon discover that he also has a creative musical snore. I can only hope that he chooses musical scores I enjoy.

Could there be a commercial opportunity in selling Snore Scores, i.e. sheet music to sleep by? Thus, instead of arguing with one's spouse or companion, he or she could simply request that one snore a chosen piece of music that evening. Thus, everyone would be content, eliminating much discord and argument in many households, perhaps even in *boat's holds*. This *notable* concept should not be immediately *scorned*—instead, it should be considered *notaboatable*.

As I walk forward through the main cabin, I feel through my legs that the boat's motion in the forward cabin is noticeably livelier than farther aft. Not good for me, as I am prone to seasickness. The halyards are slapping sharply against the aluminum mast as it sweeps from side to side in response to the rolling sea. *Diva's* erratic motion makes sleep fitful. The boat's motion and the sounds of the rigging tell me the wind is dying gradually.

As I turn in, I wonder how well we will work together as a crew, how compatible we will be, and collectively how skilled we will prove to be as sailors. As of now, I have no reason to doubt our success in this regard, but I do know that our very survival depends upon these factors. I can hear my august Danish grandmother, Ebba Rothe, saying in an unforgiving, admonitory tone, "Time will tell."

Indeed, it always does.

Saturday, 19 June 2004 – Atlantic – 2nd Day

0600 – On watch with Rob again. We are becalmed with a gossamer wind from ENE (60 degrees), velocity 1.5 knots. Nature seems as calm as Rob's temperament. The temperature on deck has already risen to 69 degrees at this early morning hour.

Our practice of relieving the helmsman every thirty minutes improves his concentration and performance. In virtually windless conditions, such as now, it must also relieve his sense of frustration. Aboard a boat the size of *Diva,* evenness of temper is the foundation of compatibility, and therefore of morale.

0740 – Becalmed, with our sails slatting about. The visibility has increased to 500 meters, revealing a dark-hulled boat to windward slightly ahead of the beam—probably the same one we saw last night.

Our Global Positioning System (GPS) shows we have traveled 3.0 nautical miles in two hours, for an average speed of 1.5 knots. This leads to some rather dismal calculations. The rhumb line distance from Beavertail Light opposite Newport to the Bermuda finish line is 635 miles. Thus, at an average speed of 5.0 knots, the trip will last 127 hours, or five days. We are now averaging 1.5 knots.

Since the CCA's Ireland cruise starts on the 15th of July, at this rate, we will be forced to drop out of the race and head directly east toward Kinsale, Ireland. We really need to put into Bermuda first, however, to top off our fuel tanks and reprovision our fresh food supply.

0850 – We are tacking, backing, turning 270 degrees. Our speed is 0.5–1.5 knots. The wind is confused and so are we. Our course swings widely between 90 degrees and 215 degrees in an effort to keep a compromise course of 165 degrees.

Rob is an excellent watchmate, a very good sailor with a cheerful, easy manner, and is an interesting conversationalist. He tells me about his extensive international travels in connection with his career in the textile machinery industry. Watches are often spent in musings and idle conservation.

Every morning, starting around 0900 hours, each boat in the fleet reports its position, as of 0800 hours, to the St. George's School's sloop *Geronimo,* which is accompanying the fleet as an observer. According to this morning's reported positions, one considerably larger Class-5 boat is only about a mile away from us.

0900 – The wind has all but disappeared. We tack four times in about ten minutes to accommodate its variable direction. Our typical sequence for finding the wind is as follows: catch a puff of wind off the port quarter by easing sails out, build up a small amount of headway causing the wind to pull ahead until we are close-winded on a beat, trim the sails accordingly until the flattened sails lose their drive and the boat slows down…until we catch another puff of wind off the quarter. Then repeat, endlessly.

0945 – Light wind, southerly at 4.0 knots. We are now beating to windward on a starboard tack, making 4–5 knots.

1000 – Garry serves a hearty, and much appreciated, breakfast of fried eggs and toast. This is an excellent start to a seafaring day.

Afterward, he decides to repair the closure fitting on my clothing locker drawer beneath my bunk. It refuses to remain secured, and slides open every time we heel. When the ocean becomes rough, my belongings will be thrown out all over the cabin, and such a mess is unacceptable according to the unspoken rules of a shipshape vessel. I assist Garry in a reconstruction effort that soon escalates into major boat surgery, involving wooden blocks, screws, drills, glue, screwdrivers, and sighting mirrors. We struggle from 1000 until 1300 hours, when we finally achieve a masterful repair of carpentry perfection—a new and useful application of Garry's neurosurgical skills.

During our lengthy labors below in the forward cabin, we are unaware that an ugly rumor has started to circulate that I have *broken drawers*. How embarrassing. Akin to Coleridge's Ancient Mariner who killed an albatross, will I be eternally becalmed and burdened by *the curse of the broken drawers*?

1330 – Howard announces that our GPS results show we have travelled 94 miles in 22 hours, for an average speed of 4.4 knots.

1800 – On watch again. I am unsettled by vaguely threatening rumors concerning an unidentified crew member's broken drawers. Bad news travels fast.

We are running wing-and-wing at 5.0 knots, with the genoa trimmed out on the spinnaker pole rigged to starboard. The wind is almost dead astern from NNW (330 deg.).

1930 – I try to call Nancy and Whit in Newport, using Howard's special mid-ocean cell phone service and manage to leave a message. Only later do I realize they are in New York City for the week. How incredibly careless of me.

2000 – Garry serves a stupendous dinner of "chicken-catch-a-tory" (sic), salad, and soup, followed by genuine ice cream with thick chocolate sauce. Good food is an important key to good morale, and Garry has provisioned *Diva* well. For that, we are all grateful.

2100 – A dense fog suddenly floods over us, reducing the visibility to 25 meters. From the cockpit, our own running lights are barely visible forward on our bow pulpit.

The wind strengthens to 10 knots and moves forward. We are now on a beam reach at 6.5–7.0 knots. *Diva* is driving ahead very comfortably, steering 170 degrees. The temperature on deck is 62 degrees, and below decks it is 70 degrees.

Sunday, 20 June 2004 –

Atlantic – 3rd Day

0200 – I sleep contentedly until I am suddenly awakened by frantic, heavy footsteps overhead. Crew members are clattering about on the foredeck. The sound of the bow wave and *Diva's* heavy rolling indicate the watch is rigging the spinnaker pole for a wing-on-wing downwind tack.

Diva is a small world in which we are all interdependent and conscious of everything each one of us is doing.

0300 – On watch. I am greeted by a glorious evening with the stars sparkling so brightly they render the Milky Way a glowing cloud illuminated by celestial searchlights. How limitless and eternal is God's realm, and how temporal and limited is ours. Gazing upon this nocturnal cosmic portrait renders it difficult to believe that we are individually significant.

Soon, a fresh wind fills in from due north (360 degrees), blowing 10–12 knots and gusting to 20 knots. We are now barreling along, dead downwind at 7.5–8.5 knots, surging to 10.5 knots. We thunder along through the seas like a fully rigged clipper ship, driving before the trade winds.

Unfortunately, the reality that we are over-canvased catches up with us. I take the helm and soon lose control of our direction by making a flying jibe. Shortly thereafter, Rob commits the same error, so we roller reef the winged genoa about 30 percent to reduce our sail area to a manageable spread.

0400 – The seas are building up to ten feet and higher with their faces becoming steeper. On the helm, I sense we are buffeted by two separate wave patterns: one from dead astern and the other from our starboard quarter.

A truly successful helmsman must have a feel for the boat, a sensitivity to the forces of wind and wave working on her. A boat is constantly telling a helmsman what she feels, communicating through movements of her deck, the direction of the wind, the set of her sails, the angle of heel (tipping), and the pressures on the ship's wheel. The ocean, wind and boat are in command, and the helmsman's objective is to maximize the boat's safety and speed.

I feel *Diva* react to this oceanic uncertainty by lifting her stern up the face of an overtaking wave until she balances on its crest. There, she hesitates and wobbles indecisively before lunging downward with a sudden burst of speed, while rolling either to windward or to leeward. As soon as she rolls, she rounds up sharply in the opposite direction of her roll. Thus, I must detect the first, subtle indication of the direction of her impending swerve and anticipate it by applying immediate and substantial counter rudder. *Diva* complicates my task by initially rolling and swerving in one direction and then reversing her tendency midway through her surging descent on the wave's backside. I must be alert to execute two opposite helm movements in quick succession, often within mere seconds of each other. My objective is simply to maintain a straight course through a turbulent ocean, thereby maximizing our speed.

This steering cycle takes about one to two minutes, occurring on average forty times per hour, or about one thousand times per day.

0700 – The other watch jibes, unfurls the genoa fully, and takes in one reef in the main. This shifts the combined center of effort of the sails slightly forward, thereby reducing our tendency to swerve, easing the helmsman's task. This also results in less wandering from our true course, yielding increased boat speed by reducing our total distance traveled through the water.

We are on the port tack with the wind slightly aft of the beam. Steady but lumpy seas, breaking at heights of six feet. Wind steady at 18 knots, and our speed is 7.5–8.2 knots.

0900 – Though *Diva* rode comfortably through last night's nasty blow, it proved disastrous to some competitors. From this morning's radio watch reports, we learn that one boat is dismasted and two have their steering gear disabled. They are all forced to power 250 miles back to Newport. Heading directly into this wind and lumpy sea must be very wet and discouraging. I imagine also the disappointment of their crews, who were anticipating a pleasant visit to Bermuda.

Last night's tempest was a good test of the soundness of our vessel and the skill of crew. The gear stood up well and the crew performed professionally. Weather permitting, we should be able to cross the North Atlantic safely, and, perhaps, even relatively comfortably.

Diva is definitely a sturdy, seaworthy vessel with solid control characteristics. She tracks well (i.e. holds her course), especially in sloppy downwind conditions. Her rudder is very large, enabling it to overpower last night's flying jibe, even against the force of the boom preventer acting as a main sheet to windward.

In contrast, I experienced a potentially disabling disaster while crossing the Atlantic in 1960 aboard Thomas J. Watson, Jr.'s *Palawan-2*. We were racing almost dead downwind across the Atlantic under spinnaker in 30-knot wind with building seas.

I witnessed the unfolding disaster from my post on the stern deck. As we started to thunder down a steep wave, our rudder lifted partially out of the water, causing our helmsman to lose directional control. *Palawan* veered to starboard, skidding sideways down the face of the wave and throwing herself onto her beam ends in the middle of the ocean. The 65-foot mast was submerged almost halfway up to her second set of spreaders. As *Palawan* rolled completely onto her side, submerging half the deck, she lifted her rudder out of the water, rendering the helm useless. The wind and the ocean had taken control completely, pinning a 30-ton, 54-foot sloop helplessly on her side, awash in breaking Atlantic waves.

I was immobilized by astonishment and fear. Thunderstruck, I fully expected the mast to break apart, possibly tearing a gaping hole in the hull, causing us to sink. I clearly remember thinking to myself, "After all this work, too bad we never made it all the way across the Atlantic." I did not have time to speculate about our personal survival in a small rubber raft in the cold North Atlantic, or whether or not anyone would hear our distress signals, or even if we would be rescued.

Somehow *Palawan* held together and gradually recovered from her prone position. The off-watch crew, which had just sat down for lunch, crowded through the hatch, rushing on deck with wild expressions of surprise and fear (Illustration 20).

At the time, I did not realize I was participating in a very significant event in the history of yachting design.

This incident merits a detailed explanation of its historic impact. In the mid-1950s, the Cruising Club of America (CCA), which sponsors the Newport–Bermuda Race, altered its measurement rules in an effort to improve yacht seaworthiness by encouraging greater beam (width) to increase lateral stability. In essence, the CCA's new rules favored broad, roomy boats with more buoyancy to withstand heavy seas and more beam to withstand heavier winds without heeling. In 1956, the famous firm of Sparkman & Stevens (S&S) designed a 40-foot yawl named *Finisterre* for the veteran yachtsman Carleton Mitchell.

Intended primarily as a comfortable cruising boat, *Finisterre* was so favored by the new CCA racing handicap rules that she won an unprecedented three Bermuda Races. In yachting circles, nothing sells like speed, so her lines were copied by virtually everyone. Thus, *Palawan-2* was a scaled up 54-foot version of *Finisterre*.

That afternoon's broaching, however, revealed a sinisterly unseaworthy aspect of our yacht's design—namely that her submerged control surfaces were inadequate for maintaining control. Without commenting at the time, Thomas J. Watson, Jr., noted this, and in 1965, he ordered *Palawan-3* from the design boards of S&S. Since he was one of their best clients, eventually ordering a total of five boats, they paid close attention to his specifications, particularly that she "track well downwind under spinnaker." Lesson learned that day, as we lay on our beam ends in the middle of the North Atlantic.

Palawan-3 was an aluminum, 58-foot racing sloop with a rather narrow, deep hull. For improved steering she had a revolutionary configuration: a rudder mounted separately on a skeg aft of her keel, which was equipped with a trim tab on its trailing edge. *Palawan-3* was an exceptionally successful racer. In 20 out of 29 races from 1966 through 1970, she placed first, second, or third, including eight times first-in-fleet and seven times first-in-class. Since then, almost without exception, yachts' rudders are mounted separately, aft of the keel.

This record was noted by S&S when they designed the famous 12-Meter *Intrepid,* which won the America's Cup twice—in 1967 in four straight races against *Dame Pattie,* and in 1970 in four out of five against *Gretel-2*.

Interestingly, the measurements of *Palawan-3* closely resemble those of a 12-Meter from the same era:

	Palawan-3	12-Meter
Length (LOA)	58	64
Waterline (LWL)	40	45
Beam	12	12
Draft	8	9
Sail Area (ft^2)	1315	1770
Displacement (tons)	23	28.5

In terms of displacement, the difference is only 19.3 percent.

Thus, our knockdown blow in the Atlantic was the initial link of this unusual chain of events. Apparently, we occasionally have unexpected hidden links with history.

19. Gulf Stream Squall (ER)

0930 – We are now 250 miles from Newport, out of a total distance of 635 miles to Bermuda. I calculate that if we can average 6.0 knots, we will arrive in 106 hours, or four days, on Wednesday the 23rd, just in time for our planned departure across the Atlantic on Friday the 25th. The probability of our averaging 6.0 knots, however, depends entirely upon our catching the Gulf Stream Eddy at the most favorable location.

In spite of the rough weather, we are warm and dry except for occasional spray on deck. The boat rolls about, making all of us use our long-dormant muscles. Their aching is just part of getting one's sea legs.

0945 – According to the fleet's reported positions, we are fairly close to the western edge of our rhumb line to Bermuda, and there is a crowd of competitors further to the west of us. Do they anticipate a strong westerly wind and are positioning themselves to catch it first, or are they looking for a boost from the meandering Gulf Stream Eddy? We regard one another with mutual suspicion. I wonder what they are saying about us.

1000 – Distance to Go (DTG) is four hundred miles, a daunting even number.

1430 – GPS navigation data reveals we are now 269 miles from the starting line at Beavertail Point, RI, with some 360 miles DTG to St. George, Bermuda. Speed Over Ground (SOG) is 8.9 knots, while our boat speed is 4.7 knots, for a net boost of 2.2 knots. These readings convince me that we have entered the deciding Gulf Stream Eddy. Let us hope our competitors to the west have missed it.

1445 – While on deck, I observe a gigantic, black finback whale about 70 feet long, cruising gracefully and silently up our starboard side on a reciprocal course about 25 meters abeam of us. I estimate his speed at about 7–10 knots. Most likely, he is enroute to meeting his girlfriend somewhere off Nantucket. If they engage in romantic activities, will they become known as tryst and Isolde?

1530 – GPS confirms that our SOG is 10.5 knots, minus our boat speed of 5.9 knots, indicating we are getting a boost of 4.6 knots from the Gulf Stream. Again, these figures confirm my suspicion that we have entered the Gulf Stream meander at the right point.

1800 – The sun is becoming noticeably stronger than it was in cloudy New England, compelling us to apply copious amounts of protective suntan lotion. All afternoon, we sail into and out of wind holes, mysterious areas where the wind does not exist. Finally, Rob and I rig the spinnaker pole to port. We manage to make every possible false lead with both the pole topping lift and the downhaul. I am glad that it is daylight and calm, knowing that this rigging practice will benefit us some dark, stormy evening.

As measured by GPS, the Gulf Stream is carrying us forward and to port, or in a slightly easterly direction. No other boats are visible, so I hope our advantage is shared with only very few competitors.

1915 – I spoke too soon. I have just spotted a boat broad on our starboard bow on the horizon, about 5–7 miles off.

After much navigational discussion, we expect to exit the Gulf Stream about 60 miles ahead of us if we maintain our present course of 170 degrees. At our present speed (SOG) of 5.8 knots and a course over ground (COG) of 165 degrees, we should exit it 10 hours from now, or at about 0400 hours tomorrow morning.

Rob has let out a long fishing line from the stern pulpit and admits that he is willing to catch any fish that is edible. To be eaten by whom?

In addition to being a fisherman, Rob reveals that he is also a dedicated global communicator. He has a daily regime whereby he throws bottles overboard containing messages written in six languages: English, Greek, Turkish, German, French, and Italian. They include much official information, including our latitude and longitude at the time of launching. It becomes quickly evident that this is a serious hobby.

At least, I believe that it is a hobby. Perhaps the increasingly strong sun is beginning to affect me, as I am unsettled by the thought: could Rob be a foreign agent? Are his bottles tagged with micro transmitters that enable them to be scooped up at night by a surfaced submarine that submerges by day in order to shadow us? Should I occasionally press my ear surreptitiously against our hull below the waterline in order to check for the sounds of the alien submarine lurking near us? To avoid discovery, I must consider my options thoroughly before acting.

2000 – Sitting with us in the cockpit during our relaxed evening conversation, Garry mentions that he performed surgery on the grandson of one of my father's closest friends. Fortunately, the operation was completely successful.

The world is surprisingly small, with only four degrees of separation in this instance. Sometimes, I wonder if we are all connected in mysterious ways we do not even detect, let alone understand.

Monday, 21 June 2004 – Atlantic – 4th Day

0001 – Standing the midwatch.

0300 – Weather is very comfortable, dry on deck, with a temperature of 67 degrees. I am wearing only long pants and a medium-weight sweater. During most ocean passages, one can go on deck only if one wears protective foul weather gear (FWG).

The wind conditions are worse than exasperating. The wind's direction varies completely, swinging from NNW (330 deg.) to NE (045 deg.). Our baseline course to our destination is 170 degrees, but our steered heading varies from 150 to 200 degrees. Our sails are set wing-on-wing with the genoa rigged on the pole to port. We are running dead downwind just to keep the sails filled and to maintain enough speed (between 1.5 to 4.5 knots) to keep steerage way. The windless condition combines with the boat's motion to cause a tremendous amount of wear on the sails and the running rigging. As they slat violently against the standing rigging, they sound like frequent detonations from a large pistol.

Brief gusts—cold from directly astern and warm from the port quarter—apparently originate from two different temperature zones of the ocean. I ask myself, "Is this frequent air temperature variation significant?"

In fact, this phenomenon combined with the variability of the winds both yesterday and today leads me to postulate *Rothe's Gulf Stream Wind Pattern* theory (Illustration 21).

My concept originated one morning in March this year, when I flew with our son, Alden, in a single-engine aircraft in the vicinity of Vero Beach, Florida. As we crossed Route I-95, a broad, four-lane highway, we experienced sudden, pronounced turbulence generated by the column of heated air over the dark pavement, even though we were at an altitude of 2,500 feet above it.

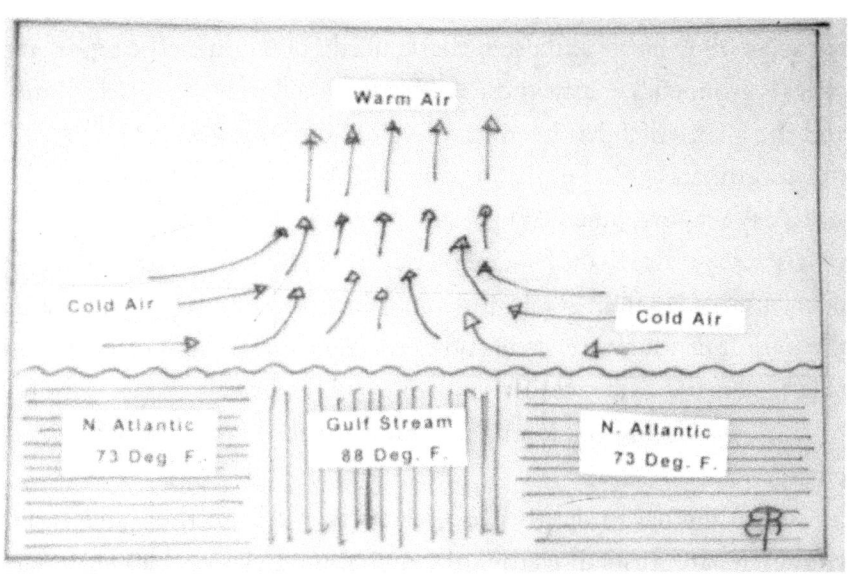

20. Rothe's Gulf Stream Wind Pattern Theory (ER)

At our present latitude of 30–40 degrees north, the Gulf Stream water temperature is about 88 degrees, while that of the surrounding Atlantic is about 73 degrees. Therefore, the warmer Gulf Stream creates thermals in the same manner as the Florida highway does, even at night. Hence, this evening we experience both cold and warm gusts of wind.

Thus, we can conclude that whenever a major wind system resulting from dominant barometric high-pressure and low-pressure areas is absent, local thermal wind patterns will prevail near the region of the Gulf Stream, and particularly along its edges.

I fully expect that these thoughts are not original; others have certainly come to the same conclusion. After all, my analysis really amounts to basic common sense. On the other hand, common sense is surprisingly uncommon.

0815 – The sloop *Geronimo* from St. George's School is accompanying the fleet as the Communications Command Vessel (CCV) for the CCA, one of the Bermuda Race sponsors. Every morning, each boat reports its position to the CCV by radio telephone, allowing all of us to monitor our competitors' positions with acute interest. The roll call begins at 0800 hours and usually lasts until 1000 hours. The reporting order is grouped by class, whereby *Geronimo* calls out the vessel's name, and the boat which has been standing by responds with its name and the coordinates of its position as of 0800 hours (Illustration 22 for yesterday's report, June 20th).

Geronimo also handles emergency reports. Last night, *Dragon's Main* hit a 55-gallon steel oil drum which was impossible to see in the dark, but fortunately she suffered only superficial damage and is able to continue the race. This morning, *Geronimo* also relays a shore-to-ship message from a family to a crewmember, reporting a medical emergency.

Regarding ocean debris, Rob relates that several thousand cargo containers are washed overboard from commercial vessels every year and float for an extended time before sinking, thus posing a fatal hazard to any sailboat having the misfortune of colliding with one of them. In effect, the container becomes a man-made iceberg, the major portion of which is submerged, thereby rendering it virtually invisible. Whether or not one hits them becomes just a question of good or bad luck.

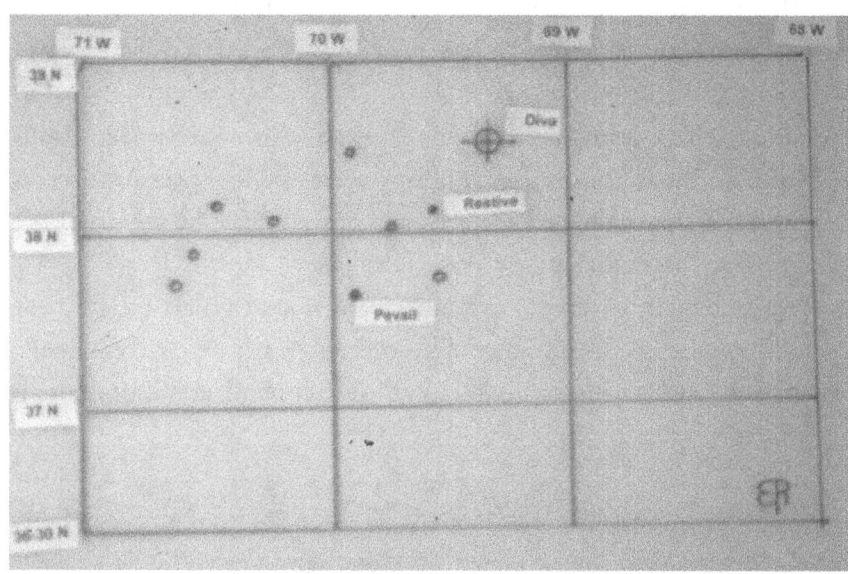

21. Class-12 Positions as of 0800 June 20th (ER)

Thinking about this possibility continuously during a long voyage could lead to a permanent state of anxiety. One alternative is best expressed by the Brown University motto: "In Deo Speramus," or, "In God We Trust." Under these circumstances, besides keeping a lookout ahead during the day, what else can a reasonable sailor do?

0830 – Wind is very light, 3–5 knots, from N (10 degrees), with slightly choppy seas. Our course is 170 degrees and our present speed is under 3.0 knots.

We are accompanied by one boat close by to port about half a mile off, another off our port bow, and one more off our starboard bow. Also, on a note of personal interest, Nancy's cousin aboard *Hound* has just reported his position at latitude 34 degrees north, while ours is 35 degrees and 53 minutes north, placing them about 100 miles ahead of us. I understand that *Hound* is a large, heavy boat, LOA 59 feet, so they are doing very well under unfavorable conditions. They probably gained quite a bit of distance during our stormy *Nantucket sleighride* early Sunday morning. Fortunately for us, they are in Class-5 and we are in Class-12.

0900 – We are racing in Class-12, for cruising canvas, with our "classmates," so to speak, listed in descending order of handicap:

1. Allegra   681
2. Counter Point   689
3. Inessa   696
4. Dragons Bane   700
5. Prevail   705
6. Reveille   705
7. Nostos   708
8. **Diva**   **708**
9. Avatar   727
10. Panache   742
11. Spirit   744
12. J'erin   750
13. Restive   760
14. Dame of Sark   794

In order to equalize a yacht's opportunity to win, each is assigned a handicap time allowance based upon the length of the race. Known as the Americap rating system, it is calculated by using a boat's measurements to determine its theoretical speed and, from that, its projected finishing time. Since *Diva* is rated in the middle of her class, we receive time from those rated above us (smaller number) and give time to those rated below us (larger number).

Many measurements are used in a complex formula to calculate a boat's rating, including LOA, LWL, beam, draft, displacement, ballast, sail area, ratio of mast height to boom length (aspect ratio), overhang, and foretriangle dimensions. Perhaps the most influential factor is the LWL, or length on the waterline, which correlates highly with a boat's maximum theoretical hull speed (MHS) in a non-planing mode. The MHS cannot be exceeded, regardless of how much sail is carried or how hard the wind propels the boat. It is the point at which resistance increases too quickly to be overcome by effort. The traditionally accepted formula for a heavy displacement boat's MHS is 1.5 times the square root of the waterline length; thus, for example, a 60-foot boat with a 49-foot waterline would have a MHS of 7 x 1.5 = 10.5 knots, when upright. When heeled, the LWL increases and so does the MHS.

Obviously, the above explanation is very oversimplified.

0915 – Wind is shifting about, ranging from dead astern to a port beam reach. The first wind direction requires us to wing out our genoa on the spinnaker pole to port, while the latter requires us to trim our genoa on a reach to starboard. Having to execute many rapid changes repeatedly in our sail trim for very little reward in gained distance is starting to frustrate and annoy us, so we devise a useful rig (see illustration 23).

Thus, we are able to shift quickly from one trim to another almost instantaneously without having to unrig the pole or even change its position. We simply roller furl the genoa and then let it out on the required side. We either haul it out on the pole on the port side using the port sheet, which slides through the fitting on the outboard end of the pole, or we simply trim the genoa to starboard using the starboard sheet. Thus, the spinnaker pole remains rigged to port, held in position by fore and after guys, in anticipation of the predictable wind shifts.

Even though this rig might be regarded as unorthodox by some, it is an innovative response to a special situation involving 90 degree wind shifts. Simply stated, in typically American terms, "It works."

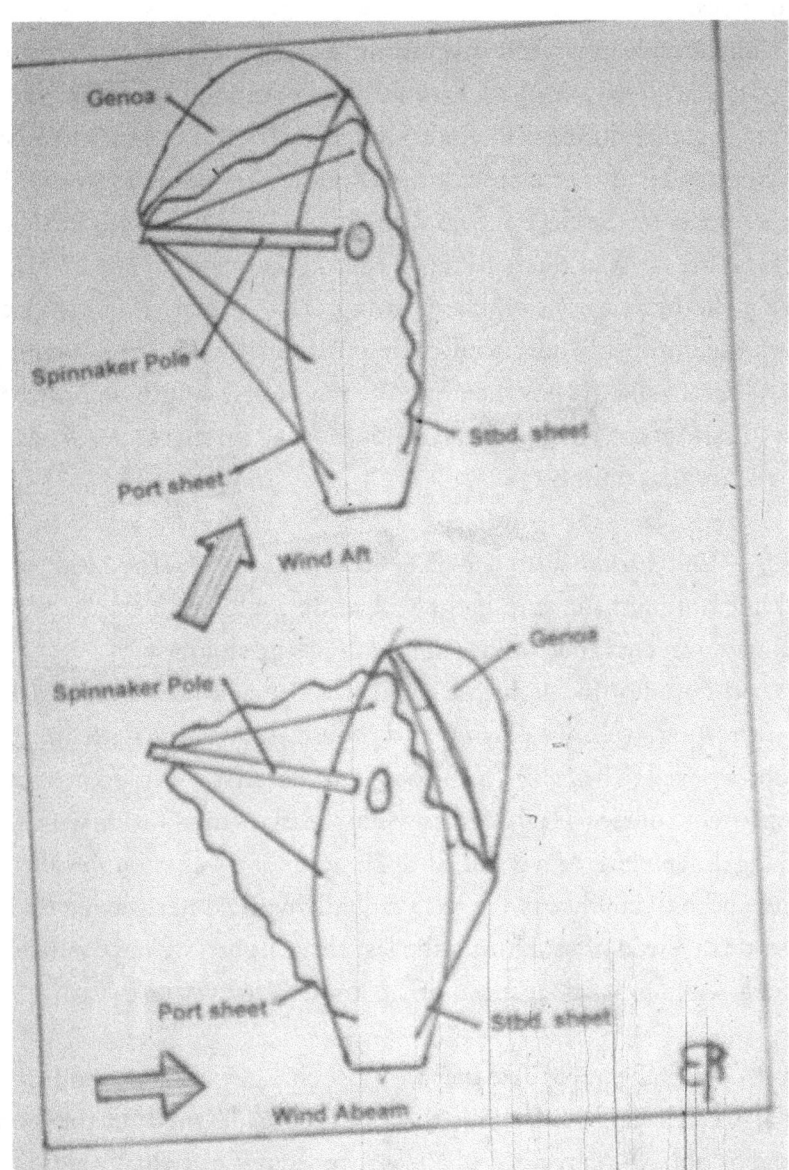

22. A Useful Rig (ER)

0940 – As we sail southward, the weather is starting to heat up noticeably. It is now 83 degrees on deck. We open all portholes and skylights, lowering the temperature below decks to a more comfortable 76 degrees.

Unbelievable news. On this morning's radio report, we learn that Class-10 has already finished. I am absolutely stunned. Both our classes started together during midafternoon of Friday 18th, and they finished on Monday 21st, for an elapsed time of under three days. How did the largest boats in the fleet accomplish this in such light weather? My guess is that most of them averaged over 20 knots for about 12 hours during the blow early Sunday morning. This nocturnal "Nantucket sleighride" probably advanced their positions by 250 to 300 miles, equivalent to slightly less than half the racecourse length, in only half a day. I cannot fully comprehend sailboat speed on that scale. What an experience that must be.

0945 – Our Distance to Go (DTG) is 251 miles. The clear skies and hot southern sun foreshadow a hot day, calling for floppy, wide-brimmed sun hats and copious amounts of suntan lotion.

Diva does not like light, variable airs, especially combined with a lumpy rolling swell. We play cat and mouse all morning with another sloop, believed to be *Pamir*, a 55-foot Swan. At first, we try to maintain a consistent course of 160 degrees while she plays the shifting winds by tacking downwind. As a result, at 0830 hours she was 0.5 miles abeam of us, and by 1200 hours she has gradually worked her way up to 1.0 miles dead ahead of us. During the last three hours, we have sailed six miles for an average boat speed of 2.0 knots. Very, very frustrating!

1200 – We finally recognize that we must change our tactics and apply our light weather sailing skills that most of us learned on the Long Island Sound, the graveyard of all boat speeds. We gradually close the gap with *Pamir* to about 250 meters, at which point we can almost see her sail numbers. During our final approach for the kill, she falls into a wind hole. Shortly thereafter, we both catch the same gossamer gust of wind and head off in different directions toward patches of more reliable winds, or so we hope. We are now *surging ahead* at 1.0–2.0 knots.

To inspire us, Garry plays a stirring Beethoven symphony on our ship's music system.

Pamir is very much larger than *Diva*, but I earnestly look forward to a rematch and to another chance to overhaul her. Our afternoon duel with *Pamir* has sharpened our sailing skills and motivated the competitive spirit in all of us, thereby improving our morale. For my part, I agree with Ralph Waldo Emerson's observation, "The pleasure of something well done, is to have done it."

Perhaps all of us should be inspired more often by our greatest hopes. If we realize only the realistic portion of them, we will accomplish far more than if we had not hoped and not tried at all. As William Shakespeare admonished in *Julius Caesar*,

"There is a tide in the affairs of men,
Which, taken at the flood, leads on to fortune,
Omitted, all the voyage of their life
Is bound in shallows and in miseries."

1400 – On course at 160 degrees, speed 3.0 knots. The finish line bears 159 degrees at a distance of 250 miles. At this rate, we will finish in about 80 hours, or three days, late on Thursday. Will we be forced to drop out of the race beforehand, in order to turn northeast toward Ireland? I am deeply disappointed by the thought of not having a fair chance to beat *Pamir*, and everyone else in our class, for that matter, because of unusually calm weather. To paraphrase a traditional saying, *sailors propose, the weather gods dispose*.

The sky is transparently clear, the ocean a reflective, deep, cobalt blue, and both are ideal except for the accompanying fiery sun. I am wearing a T-shirt, long trousers for sun protection, and a wide-brimmed safari style hat. Temperatures are 97 degrees on deck and 83 degrees below decks. We rig the cockpit awning to provide a comfortable, shaded refuge.

1500 – I examine our plot of today's 0800 fleet positions (see illustration 24), which confirms that *Pamir* is our dueling competitor. Our competitive situation in our class appears quite favorable.

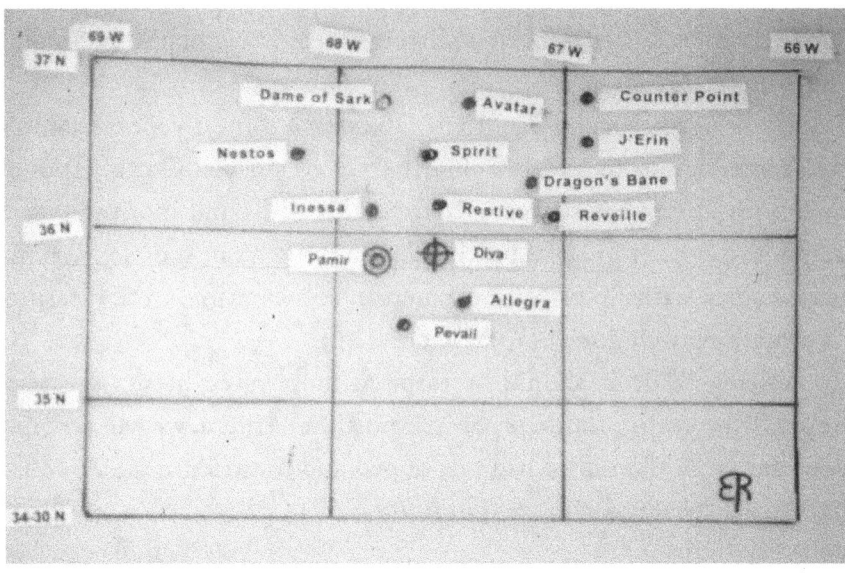

23. Class-12 Fleet Positions June 21st (ER)

1600 – *Unbelievable luxury.* I enjoy a freshwater shower with both hot and cold running water. What a miracle at sea.

Diva's freshwater machinery makes this luxury possible by extracting 15 gallons per hour of fresh water from the salty ocean. The boat's auxiliary engine drives a very high-pressure pump that forces seawater through a series of micro-fine membranes that filter out the salt molecules. The discharged water is fresh, truly a product of technological magic.

My shower even includes a shampoo. Forty-four years ago, such luxuries were unknown, even on the largest yachts, including *Palawan*. Back then, we carried all our fresh water with us across the Atlantic and rationed every gallon very carefully, using it only for drinking and cooking. We were permitted to wash our face and hands in freshwater occasionally, but that was the extent of our personal hygiene. *Palawan* carried a total of 240 gallons of fresh water—170 gallons in the ship's tanks, plus an additional 70 in plastic, five-gallon jugs carried on deck. For 10 men and an anticipated voyage duration of 25 days, this supply provided a total daily allowance of 10 gallons, equivalent to one gallon per man per day for all uses—principally, for cooking.

In those days, it was difficult to observe the adage, *cleanliness is next to godliness.*

1630 – We are becalmed, slatting about on glassy rolling waves beneath a relentless sunshine. This is genuine skin cancer weather. Our speed, if you can call it that, is 1.4 knots. *Diva* prefers a fresh breeze, and so do we.

As I make my way about on a pitching, rolling boat, I must use my arms to steady myself by hanging onto various fixtures and surfaces. I now sense that my muscles are toning up, since I feel less worn out after each watch and experience less soreness and stiffness. Last night, however, I suffered from excruciating leg cramps from hitherto unused muscles. I am told that tonic water cures this.

1700 – Regrettably, we do not celebrate a daily *happy hour* aboard *Diva*. Our skipper seems *Bligh*-thly indifferent to this issue. After all, even the British Navy serves grog.

1915 – Sea of glass. Our speed is 0.0 knots. I am not kidding. The gauge actually reads "0.0."

1930 – I temporarily overcome my instinctive aversion to the ship's stove and, with Rob's help, I cook a substantial seafaring dinner consisting of spaghetti, vegetable soup, fruit, cookies, etc. Will I eventually lose my desire to avoid the ship's galley? Perhaps when we sail further north across the Atlantic into cold, hostile climes, galley duty will appear more attractive than freezing and being soaked while on watch on deck.

2100 – Now on watch. I am awed by a spectacular starry night with celestial orbs so bright I can almost perceive their round forms. No mere points of light, they appear as the very eyes of heaven. The Milky Way glows in a wide arc across the heavens like a giant cloud of luminous dust. A sliver of moon slowly fades to orange and sinks silently into the sea. How great is God's universe, and how small is our personal portion of it. How can some of us believe that we are its only intelligent inhabitants? What asinine conceit. Perhaps these people also believe that the world is flat.

2120 – Wonderfully comfortable evening with a temperature of 73 degrees. The boat is completely dry topsides, so I feel comfortable wearing long pants and a sweater. The wind is S (180 degrees) at 1.0–5.0 knots. Our course is 135–145 degrees, and our speed is 1.0–3.0 knots.

I call Nancy, AKA *Mariposa,* at home in New York City using Howard's special transoceanic cell phone. She is astounded by my unexpected call and reports that all is fine at home. I am grateful for that. An accomplished sailor in her own right, she appreciates our favorable fleet position and hopes that we will not have to drop out for lack of wind to power into Bermuda for provisioning. She enjoys my tale of our duel with *Pamir* and wishes us good luck. I am very grateful for the miracle of modern communication that enables me to talk directly with my dearest Mariposa from a starry night in the Atlantic Ocean.

2245 – As I am sitting in the cockpit gazing at the heavens in the northeast, I notice a peculiarly errant star. It travels erratically across the sky, stopping and starting instantaneously, and moving back and forth on various courses and speeds. It looks like a shining, wingless house fly buzzing about the heavens. This activity lasts about a minute or two until its light fades abruptly from sight. I estimate that this wandering luminous object traverses an area measuring about 10–15 degrees vertically and an equal amount horizontally, and that the maneuvering zone is located about forty degrees above the horizon (Illustration 25).

I remember that, according to a college psychology class on visual perception, if a single spot of light is shone onto a wall in a completely darkened room without other visible reference points, it appears to move. This evening's observations are not the case, however, since the errant star is surrounded by a multitude of stars with fixed positions relative to each other. Thus, the object must be moving in relation to the other stars. Most unusual! How strange!

I weigh three possible explanations:

First, I have just witnessed an unusual celestial event, such as the implosion of a star, in a distant galaxy. As the star disintegrates, alternating chains of volcanic eruptions act like giant rocket engines propelling it wildly about the heavens.

Second, a space vehicle's computer has malfunctioned, causing its rocket engines to fire chaotically, thrusting it on random courses about the sky.

Third, a microscopic luminous insect, such as a miniature firefly, has crawled across the lens of my eyeglasses and then taken flight.

Well, I must admit that there is also a fourth explanation…but that is best left to the aficionados who devotedly monitor a secret Airforce base in Area 51, near Roswell, New Mexico. Are we connected with unknown parties whom we do not yet perceive, in ways we do not understand?

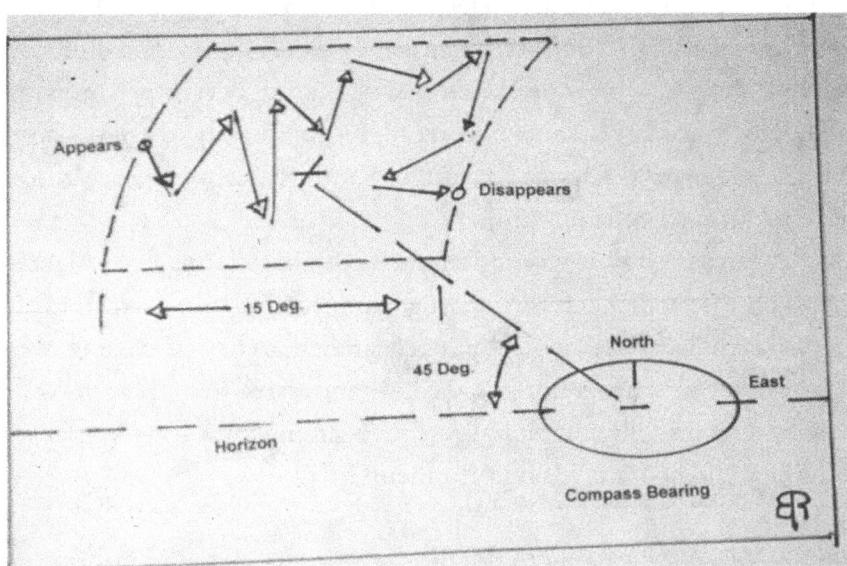

24. Ernst's Errant Star (ER)

2330 – We turn on the autopilot briefly to test it before our transatlantic crossing. To our wonderment, we discover that *Diva* really is quite a woman, and a very sexy, sultry one at that. Whenever the hydraulic system mechanically activates the rudder, we hear distinct sounds resembling moans of female sexual pleasure. How are we expected to sleep through the night listening to this amorous aria?

Tuesday, 22 June 2004 – Atlantic – 5th Day

0600 – On watch. It is a clear, sunny day, almost cloudless. Extremely light and variable winds, ESE (115 degrees), 2–4 knots. Our course is 175 degrees and our speed about 3.0 knots.

After a long discussion of presidential politics, our consensus is that President George W. Bush's reelection is very much in doubt. (He subsequently won by a comfortable margin.) Our conversation shifts to Ronald Reagan, who is perceived as a very kind, decent person with a vivacious sense of humor. As I recall, when asked by the press how his discussions with Desmond Tutu of South Africa were proceeding, Reagan grinned and said, "So, so!"

Reagan passed away recently after ten years of suffering from Alzheimer's Disease, which left him staring blankly ahead, removed from all personal contact. Apparently, on his deathbed, as he was passing over to the other side, he sat upright abruptly and stared directly at his wife Nancy with his fully conscious presence beaming forth from his eyes.

What did he see in his final moments?

0830 – Garry is listening to the fleet position reports and informs us that, of the 38 boats in our vicinity, we are ahead of 12 of them (Illustration 26).

0900 – After we ghost along at 2–3 knots for several hours, the wind suddenly shifts to SSE (150 degrees) and fills in to 5–6 knots. We trim to port tack, then tack to starboard to our course of 100 degrees. We then tack back to port and are now steering 205–220 degrees with a speed of 5.5 knots. The wind appears to be filling in solidly. Our base course is still 165 degrees.

We expect southerly winds, shifting to SW and gradually strengthening. The wind varies direction about 20 degrees with each puff.

According to our GPS, we appear to have a slight lee bow on the starboard tack, so we plan to favor the western side of the rhumb line to pick up any southwester that may fill in. We are now being headed, so eventually we expect to tack onto port.

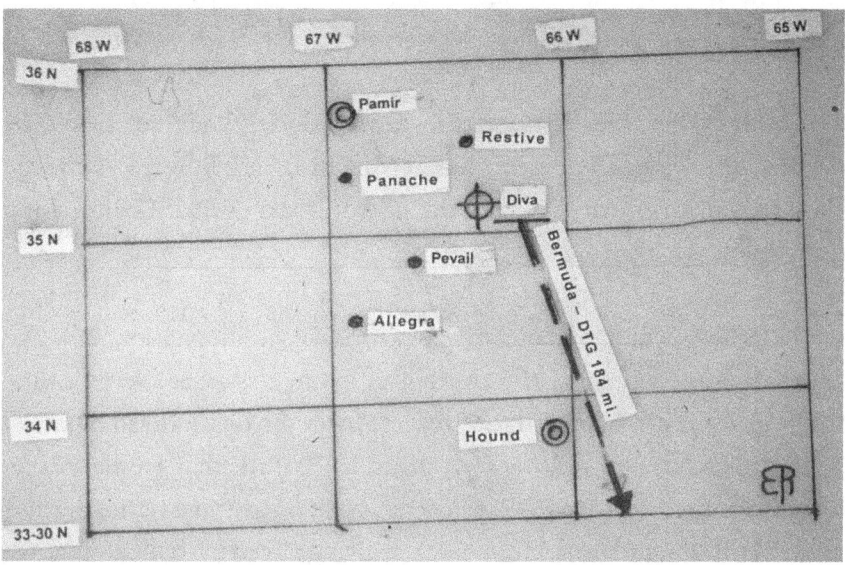

25. Class-12 Positions as of 0800 June 22nd (ER)

Our present heading is SSW (235 degrees) and our boat speed is 5.5–6.1 knots. To maximize our speed, we reluctantly roll up the cockpit awning, thereby sacrificing its enjoyable shade.

We discuss barracudas at considerable length and conclude that they are attracted to shiny objects, such as watches, necklaces, etc. Since women wear jewelry, does this mean that men's prehistoric ancestors were barracudas, that evolved and emerged from the sea? Where did they come ashore? Wall Street?

One of our crew recounts a tale that gives us unique insight into the history of *Geronimo*, the St. George's School yacht. Her famous school afloat program was run for many years by Captain Steve Connet and his wife, both of whom understood teenagers especially well. According to one tale, at the outset of every voyage, he would teach new crew members the importance of maintaining one's balance on board a boat. It was his custom to moor the boat Mediterranean style with the stern to the pier, rigged with a narrow gangplank for boarding. Everyone ashore was required to be back aboard by the evening curfew of 2100 hours. At that hour, having returned earlier, the veteran crew members would sit quietly on deck in the dark and watch the novices climbing aboard, cheering loudly whenever anyone fell into the harbor. This certainly was a "stern" lesson in sobriety.

1000 – Off watch. Temperatures are: on deck 73 degrees, below 79 degrees, and water 83 degrees. It is getting discernibly hot, so I change to shorts for comfort. We open the portholes to induce a comforting draft below decks.

1015 – We plot our daily fleet position (see illustration 26). We appear to be in contention for third place in our class, since we give time to the boats astern of us and receive time from the boats ahead of us.

Pamir is now 14 miles astern of us, so I think that we have won our duel rather decisively. Since we are both heavy-air boats of rather classic hull design and racing under cruising canvas, I believe that we sailed *Diva* well while challenged by varying conditions requiring many changes of course and sail trim. As the wind steadies and freshens, *Pamir's* greater length of 55 feet and her longer waterline will give her enough of a speed advantage to overhaul us. Not even as talented a crew as we or as fine a vessel as *Diva* can overcome the universal and eternal laws of hydrodynamics.

Nancy's cousin, Frank Eberhart, aboard his 59-foot sloop *Hound* in class-5, appears to be doing well and is now a daunting 100 miles ahead of us. With an estimated DTG of 84 miles and a probable speed of 7 knots under weather conditions like ours, *Hound* should finish in about 12 hours, or before midnight tonight—just in time for the crew to go below for a celebratory libation.

1030 – Our DTG is 184 miles. Since 2400 hours yesterday, we have sailed 32 miles in 10 hours for an average speed of 3.2 knots. At this rate, we will finish in 2.5 days. Time is tight.

So far on this voyage, we have not seen very much sea life—only one whale, six porpoises, two petrels, a few flying fish, and the usual

Portuguese man o' war jellyfish. With their rigid spines rigged as sails, occasionally even they seem to be moving faster than we are. The present lack of ocean life contrasts dramatically with its abundance during my 1960 crossing, and I find this unexpected change very unsettling. Is this a trend? Is mankind's intervention in nature's balance causing wildlife's extinction in some manner? I am very unhappy about this possibility.

I enjoy sitting below on the comfortable settee in the commodious main cabin, reading and writing, followed by a nap.

1230 – During lunch preparation by two crew members, who shall remain anonymous, one relates how his granddaughter spat her food out onto the floor, and when he admonished her, she rushed off to her mother, complaining of her grandfather's cruelty. Fortunately, we do not have such a disciplinary problem aboard *Diva*—undoubtedly, because our food is so good.

1400 – Perfect afternoon sail with the wind SSW, 10 knots, sailing 170 degrees on our rhumb line course of 163 degrees at 7.7 knots, steering semi-close hauled on the starboard tack. DTG is 170 miles, so at this rate our Estimated Time of Arrival (ETA) is Wednesday evening. With only one day of scheduled layover, our timing is getting very tight. I feel an undercurrent of rising tension.

1645 – Wind is SSW (200 degrees) at 10–12 knots. Our course is 170 degrees, and our speed is 7.1 knots. We are close hauled on the starboard tack.

Garry and I have a lengthy cockpit discussion of why the wind always appears to be stronger elsewhere when one is becalmed. In other words, distant water appears darker, more ruffled by wind, than closer water in the foreground. We develop two strikingly opposite theories.

My more technical theory is based upon optics (Illustration 27). I have noticed that the tops of the waves are comparatively darker in color than the troughs. Also, when viewed from different angles, parallel lines produce different appearances that result in contrasting colors. Since parallel waves in the viewer's foreground (A-1) are seen from the top down, they appear further apart. The resultant lighter color of the troughs predominates, which is interpreted as a lack of wind. In contrast, parallel waves further away (A-2) appear closer together and the darker color of the tops predominates. As a result, the viewer assumes that the darker color results from more wind rather than from a different angle of viewing.

Garry's theory involves the interrelationship between illusion, desire, and reality. He postulates that most of our desires, especially distant ones, are illusions. As we approach them, reality intrudes, converting them into a less desirable state. Thus, distant winds appear more desirable than the actual ones at hand.

To this extent, I must agree with him that when one is becalmed, one wishes that one were somewhere else—in fact, anywhere else.

2100 – On watch. The wind is SW (225 degrees) at 10–12 knots, and we are on a close reach to starboard, with a course of 170 degrees and a speed of 7.8 knots. Temperatures are 80 degrees on deck and 82 degrees below deck.

2400 – Off watch.

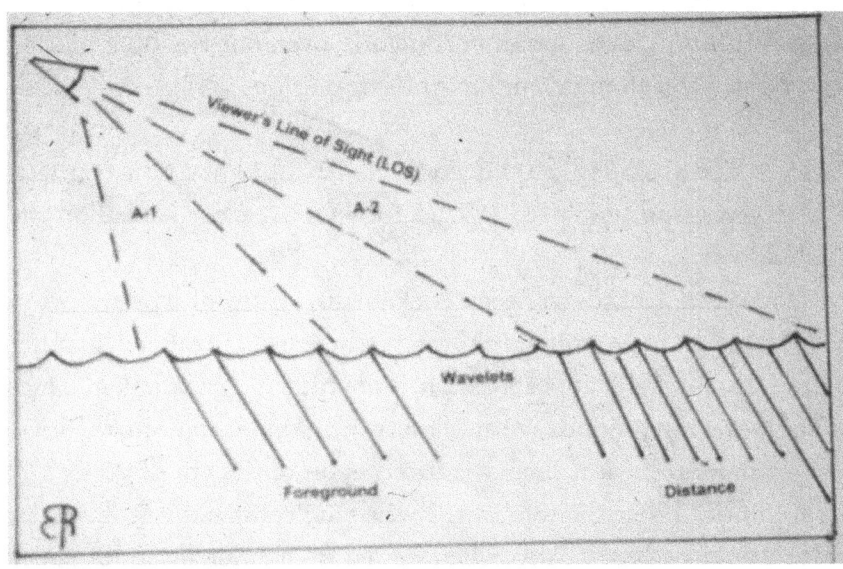

26. Rothe's Theory of Ruffled Water Optics (ER)

Wednesday, 23 June 2004 – Atlantic – 6th Day

0300 – On watch.
    Wind: SW 225 degrees S 10–12 knots (speed).
    Boat: C-165 degrees (course), S-7.5–8.83 knots (speed)
    Calm, no swells, temperature on deck 77 degrees and below decks 77 degrees

We are sailing on a close reach, a very pleasant change from slatting about under windless conditions. I am wearing a sweater and long pants. It is dry on deck with no seas splashing aboard over the bow. The wind dies slightly and then picks up again. We see no boats' navigation lights astern.

The Bermuda weather station forecasts winds hauling from SW to W and increasing to 15–20 knots this afternoon, then to 25–30 knots this evening with scattered rain showers.

0600 – Off watch. Our DTG is 61 miles. At an average speed of 7.5 knots, we have 8.5 hours remaining for an ETA of 1430 at the finish line off northeastern Bermuda (see page 85 for our actual finishing time).

I am becoming more concerned about the second leg of our journey to Ireland. To take advantage of today's strengthening breeze, can we arrive in time to clean up and provision the boat in order to depart half a day early on Thursday the 24th?

1100 – The wind is WSW (242 deg.) and has freshened to 15 knots, as predicted. Partly overcast, otherwise clear with good visibility.

Frankly, I will be happy when this race is over. The windless slatting about and drifting our way to Bermuda has been very wearing on the crew, as well as on the boat and gear. Regardless, the crew has hidden its anxiety and maintained its morale very well. This morning's position report indicates that we are among the first five boats in our class, and possibly a contender for third place. Our DTG is 20 miles to Kitchen's Shoals, which is about four miles from the finish line located off of St. David's Head on the easternmost point of Bermuda (see illustrations 28 and 29).

Garry talks to Angela this morning and reports that Nancy will be in New York City until Thursday, tomorrow evening.

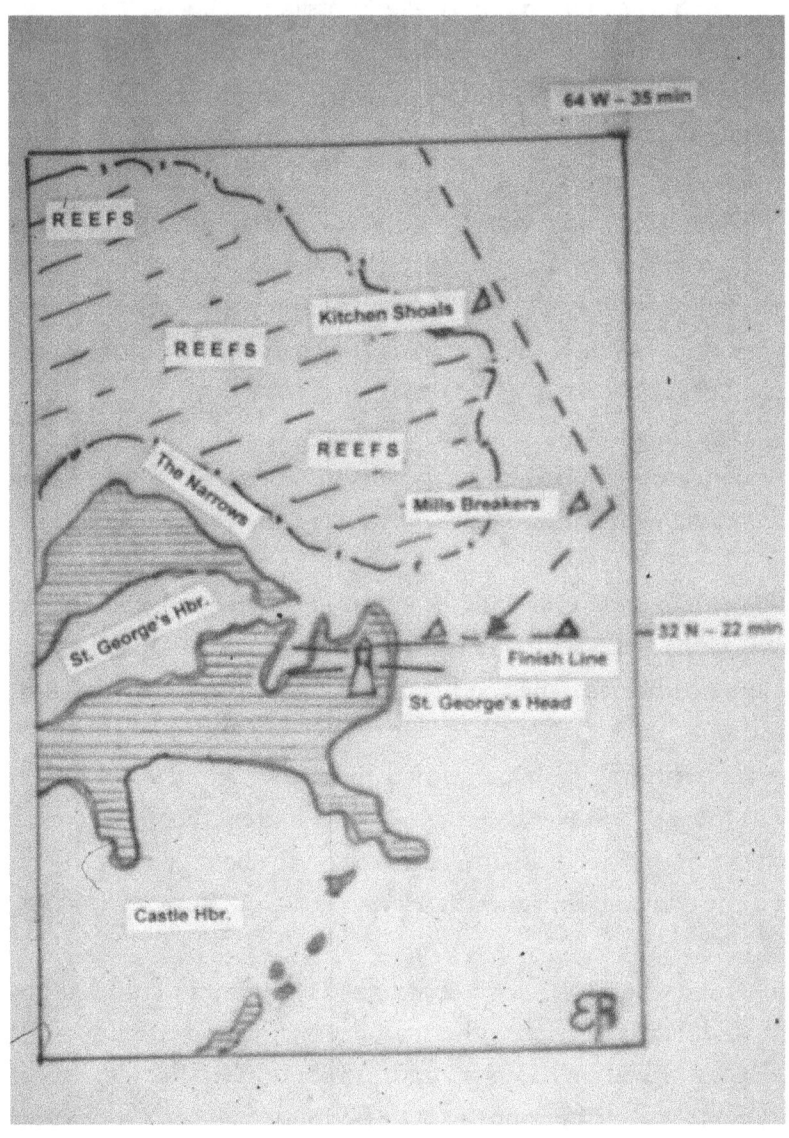

27. 28 Approaches to Bermuda (Chart) (ER)

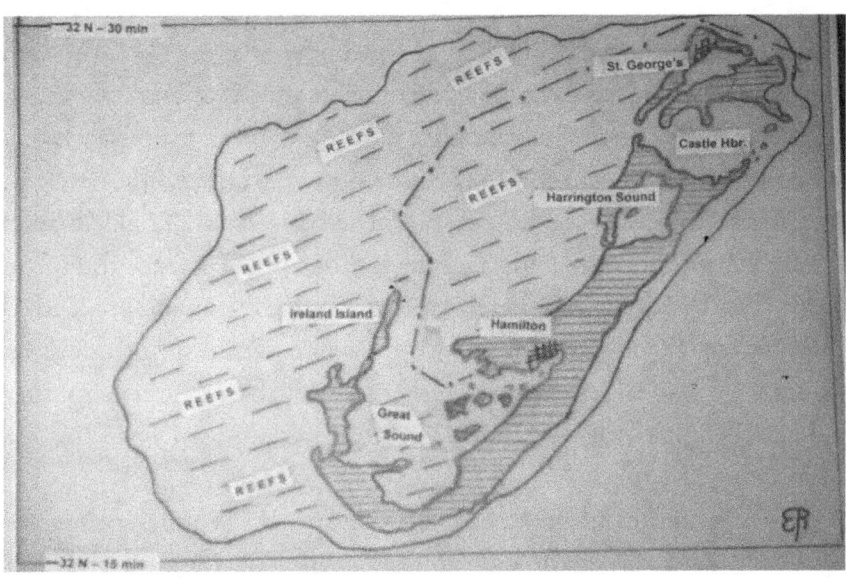

28. Greater Bermuda (Chart) (ER)

Bermuda is the remnant top of an extinct volcano. I certainly hope that it *remains* extinct during our visit.

Bermuda's dry land is formed by the southeastern sector of the cone's edge, while the remaining submerged portion forms a spacious ring of dangerous coral reefs. These treacherous waters should be traversed only by experienced mariners using accurate charts that incorporate comprehensive, useful navigational details.

My two attached charts are prime examples of my cartographic skills, or my lack thereof.

1315 – I come on deck to witness our crossing the finish line. The wind from WSW has freshened to 20 knots with gusts to 25 knots, as predicted. There, off the starboard bow to windward, lies the glorious sight of Bermuda! A glistening white and green haven in a foaming blue sea.

1330 – Mill's Breakers are to starboard. On our final approach to the line, we head up slightly, take a reef in on the main, and trim the genoa, requiring heroic grinding by Howard and me. I feel that *Diva* is still a bit overpowered and that we also should reef the genoa with 2–3 turns on the headstay.

1403 – At 14 hours, 3 minutes, and 3 seconds, we cross the finish line with St. David's Head light on a line of bearing of 191 degrees.

Well, we finally finished, after five days. Now, on to the next voyage.

As we approach the entrance to the outer harbor channel, we roll up the genoa and tack to port toward The Narrows channel. At buoy number 2 we drop the main and start the engine to enter the inner harbor. We hoist our Q-signal flag for quarantine status and proceed to the Customs Dock. Fortunately, we receive the enthusiastic dockside assistance of a local resident who paces the length of the pier shouting helm and engine orders to Garry, liberally interlaced with profanities.

1530 – We venture ashore to discover that confusion and bureaucratic disorder reign between the Customs Office in St. George and the head office in Hamilton. Apparently, we must proceed to Hamilton to clear customs. Because using the inside channel route requires detailed local knowledge which we do not have, I foresee that we will have to spend at least six hours transiting the outer route. I know this because I did it on *Palawan*. Fortunately, we finally are permitted to tie up in St. George in quarantine while Garry takes a car to Hamilton to present our documents there. What an annoying climax to our sailing adventure.

Why doesn't the Bermudian government simply maintain two separate customs clearance offices? How simple. How obvious, especially since cruise ships call regularly at St. George. Why do so many governments lack simple common sense?

1630 – We proceed to our berth at Captain Smoke's marina. Garry maneuvers masterfully in a strong wind from the starboard beam, backing into our dock to moor stern-to-the-dock in the Mediterranean manner. On these occasions, it certainly helps to have a powerful engine, and ours is a seventy-five horsepower diesel.

Our gangplank is attached to our stern pulpit at one end and rests on the dock at the other, which is 5 to 8 feet above the water, depending upon the tide. The plank is only one foot wide and spans about 6 feet, shifting about as the boat moves restlessly at her mooring. Since I am intimidated by heights, the plank becomes an unwelcome psychological obstacle to my going ashore.

1730 – We adjust our watches one hour ahead to the local time. Howard's girlfriend Doris and her friend Maryanne arrive, and the three of them (referred to collectively as Howard & Company) promptly disappear ashore. Garry plans to take our passports and papers to the Royal Bermuda Yacht Club (RBYC) desk in Hamilton, but we learn that there is a general taxi strike. What a run of lousy luck.

1830 – We all take showers, then Garry departs for Hamilton with a privately hired driver while John, Rob, Neil, and I set forth in search of drinks and dinner—which we find at Tavern-by-the-Sea. We enjoy a very congenial evening of wide-ranging conversation. I treat myself to a gin and tonic—much needed, after a long voyage from Newport—followed by a dinner of curried shrimp with coconut and rice, French vanilla ice cream, and a glass of white wine. As the French correctly maintain, "A meal without wine is like a day without sunshine."

2100 – Garry finds us at the restaurant, and we collectively treat him to dinner. On board *Diva*, he often attempts to simplify our menus by offering the crew only one choice. Now, we respond by forcing him to accept our only offer: "You eat dinner only if we pay." The restaurant manager agrees, so Garry graciously accepts.

Garry informs us that we are in contention for third place in our class. I am extremely pleased for him and for all of us. This is quite an achievement for *Diva,* which is not a skinned-out boat for ghosting along in light airs. She is solidly built, very seaworthy, and needs moderate-to-strong winds to get her rolling. In short, she is the ideal vessel for the ocean crossing ahead of us.

Our dinner conversation analyzing the race leads to some conclusions:

(A) We probably entered the Gulf Stream Meander at just the right point, and as a result, we were carried southward at 3.5–4.5 knots for 15 to 20 hours. At an average boost of 4.0 knots for 17 hours, our relative position would have been advanced some 70 miles ahead of our competition outside the current. Interestingly, others in our vicinity, such as *Pamir*, should have enjoyed the same advantage, but we left them astern.

(B) In spite of our shared wind conditions, we were able to move about 15 miles ahead of her in the course of 24 hours before the strong SW breeze filled in. Both *Pamir* and *Diva* are heavily built boats suitable for heavy weather, but *Pamir*, a Swan-55, is significantly larger and faster when the wind blows. Therefore, it is fair to say that we handled *Diva* well in calm weather, particularly with regard to helmsman issues, such as choice of correct course-to-wind in order to maximize our boat speed while maintaining the shortest course to the finish line.

Factor (A) is luck, while factor (B) is skill. We were able to take advantage of both to achieve a respectable showing. I am happy for Garry that we have done well enough to be in contention for a prize, and I am proud of us for having achieved that.

It has also become clear to me that Garry has selected an especially fine crew of experienced, capable sailors who work smoothly as a team. They are all cheerful, helpful, responsive, and polite to one another, creating a very strong sense of interdependence coupled with mutual respect. Appropriately, whenever anyone accomplishes a notable task, the individual immediately shares credit with other team members. Our attitude is always "we," not "I."

Frankly, selecting a crew of such fine character reflects well on Garry's leadership, and he has made *Diva* a very special boat on which any deep water sailor would be proud to serve.

I am very content, and am looking forward to our passage across the North Atlantic with a sense of quiet confidence.

Bermuda – An Ocean Outpost

Our race ends in Bermuda, located 635 miles southeast of Newport, Rhode Island.

This isolated island was discovered by accident in 1503 by the Spanish explorer Juan de Bermudez when he was shipwrecked here. Named after him, Bermuda consists of a total of 150 islands, of which twenty are inhabited and only six are considered important. The capital city, Hamilton, is located on the main island of Great Bermuda, which is 23 kilometers (14 miles) long. The estimated total population in 2004 was 65,000 inhabitants, of which about 60 percent are of African descent.

Bermuda's mild climate (with average temperatures of 64 degrees F in winter and 79 degrees in summer) and the island's proximity to New York and other large cities on the US East Coast make it a prime vacation resort. Over 280,000 tourists visited it in 2002, but Bermuda was not always so popular.

Throughout the 1500s, Bermuda was shunned because passing mariners heard the cries of thousands of Bermuda petrels and believed it to be inhabited by demons. The islands were used occasionally as a refuge by French privateers but remained unsettled.

In 1609, the London-based merchant syndicate known as the Virginia Company dispatched Admiral Sir George Somers in command of a fleet of nine vessels to rescue their foundering colony in Jamestown, Virginia, established on the banks of the James River in 1607. Having set forth from Plymouth, England, the fleet was within seven days of reaching Cape Henry in Virginia when they were overwhelmed by hurricane-strength winds from a tempestuous Northeaster. Their flagship, *Sea Venture,* was swept between the reefs near St. George and ran aground a short distance offshore. All 150 men and women made it to the beach without loss of life. The unexpected settlers found the island heavily forested with cedars and palmettos and inhabited by birds and wild hogs. They discovered immediately that, having neither wells nor natural reservoirs, Bermuda's only source of freshwater is rain. During the next nine months, the settlers built two new ships, *Deliverance* and *Patience,* from local wood and the timbers of *Sea Venture* in order to complete their voyage. Their saga became the inspiration for Shakespeare's *The Tempest*.

In 1612, the Virginia Company formed a subsidiary called the Bermuda Company and sent 60 settlers to establish the first permanent colony at St. George. Initially, the economy involved activities connected with whaling, cedar, and salt, as well as the cultivation of potatoes, cabbages, onions and tobacco, which was their principal export to England. Because of poor quality and import taxes, this trade declined until 1712 when Bermuda started to import tobacco.

The Bermudians, however, have a special aptitude for survival through independence of action, flexibility of tactic, and recognition of opportunity. Consequently, they soon realized their unique circumstances rendered agriculture an unpromising activity. Instead, they began to take advantage of their mid-ocean location by engaging in a trading triangle, consisting of Bermuda, the West Indies, and the Continental Colonies. The growing Bermudian maritime activity prompted them to establish several shipyards that utilized the locally grown cedars to build about thirty *sloops* annually. Their vessels achieved such a reputation for durability and speed that they were frequently used for piracy and privateering, which flourished in the Caribbean. The local merchants extended their range of services by also provisioning their customers' ships in St. George harbor. Not content to be mere spectators, local captains established their own lucrative raiding operations against homeward bound merchant ships from Spain and France.

In 1663, the arrival of the first tourist—the Rev. Michael Wigglesworth from Malden, Massachusetts—was recorded. In 1684, the British government assumed the charter from the Bermuda Company.

During the American Revolution, the Continental Congress's trade embargo with England included Bermuda and deprived it of its primary source of food, threatening its very survival. A desperate delegation's pleas for relief in exchange for unlimited supplies of salt were rejected until they offered to substitute gunpowder. An accelerated shipment of powder from Bermuda was used by George Washington to drive the British out of Boston, and the embargo was lifted.

In the early 1800s, British naval power in the North Atlantic was secured by three naval bases and shipyards in Halifax, Antigua, and Bermuda, strategically located to provide immediate support to the fleet. During the War of 1812, considerable numbers of American slaves sought refuge onboard British ships that brought them to Bermuda, where they were employed as free craftsmen in the local shipyards. After the war, many emigrated to Trinidad. In 1815, Bermuda's capital was moved from St. George to Hamilton. In 1834, slavery was abolished throughout Britain and its colonies.

When the American Civil War broke out in 1861, the Union blockade of southern ports rendered direct trade between the Confederacy and Europe impossible. As a result, strong family and commercial ties between Bermudians and prominent families in the coastal southern states caused St. George harbor to be used for transshipment of cargo carried by European merchant ships and Confederate blockade runners. The old Globe Hotel on King's Square in St. George became the headquarters of the Confederacy's chief political agent. Once again, Bermudian flexibility and opportunism had served their self-interest, as local trade profits increased ten-fold. Unfortunately for the local merchants, the lucrative trade collapsed in January, 1865, when Fort Fisher in North Carolina fell to Union forces.

In 1874, the Bermuda government signed a contract with the Quebec Steamship Company to establish regular service between New York and Bermuda, only 211 years after the arrival of the first tourist, Rev. Wigglesworth. In 1883, Princess Louise, the daughter of Queen Victoria, visited the island, and the Pembroke Hotel was renamed in her honor. Even though Mark Twain described Bermuda as "an earthbound heaven," the tourist industry did not become an important economic factor until 1912, when the government tourist bureau mounted a publicity campaign to dispel the general ignorance regarding the island paradise. According to one story, one elderly London gentleman remarked to another that "Bermuda is our stronghold in the Pacific." In 1937, tourism received another boost from the initiation of scheduled seaplane service from New York City.

During the World War II Lend Lease Agreement, the United States acquired the 99-year rights to 500 acres, on which they built Kindley

Airforce Base and a naval air station. Bermuda served as an important base for extended, mid-ocean, anti-submarine air patrols that were crucial to defeating the German U-Boats.

Following the war, in 1946, Pan American Airways began regular flights from New York City to Kindley Field. In 1959, NASA built a tracking station on Cooper's Island which served as a key communications link when Apollo 11 made the first manned lunar landing in July 1969.

In the 1960s, Bermuda experienced its share of political turbulence and public reform movements. In 1963, the Progressive Labor Party (PLP) was formed to represent the predominantly African-descent working class, while the United Bermuda Party (UBP) was established to serve the opposition. In 1966, the Parliamentary Election Act was enacted, granting the voting power to every British subject older than 21 years of age who had resided in Bermuda for a minimum of three years. In 1970, the Bermuda pound was replaced by the decimal Dollar, pegged to the US dollar.

During the 1980s, tourism reached a high-water mark and gradually began to share its economic prominence with rapidly growing financial services industries, such as banking, insurance, and offshore corporate headquarters. Bermuda offered its legal and financial independence as a lucrative incentive to corporations, serving as a Mid-Atlantic Switzerland. Office space in Hamilton doubled within a decade, and Bermudians' traditional flexibility and opportunism served their self-interest well. Once again, they have succeeded by looking overseas for their prosperity. Well done, for a small island community.

In the early 1970s, and again in August 1995, an Independence Referendum was soundly defeated at the polls in a bitterly divisive campaign, and Bermuda retained its traditional ties with Great Britain.

Today, tourism remains Bermuda's most visible activity. As a New Yorker, I am greatly amused by the posters in Bermuda advertising vacation trips to New York City. So much in life depends upon one's point of view.

Thursday, 24 June 2004 – St. George, Bermuda

0900 – John, Neil, and I commence a thorough wash-down and general clean-up of the boat, a task that lasts until 1030 hours. Rob and Garry go ashore to secure provisions. Upon their return, *Diva's* evident cleanliness is appreciated and even praised. Perhaps my training at the US Naval Officers' Candidate School in Newport has finally paid off, forty-one years later. Rob comments, "Our taxpayers' dollars have been wisely invested." I take that as a rare compliment from a frugal Rhode Islander.

As we are working, we cannot avoid noticing a strikingly attractive, tall, brunette, female captain on the sloop moored alongside. She tells us that several days earlier, when she was maneuvering alongside the dock, she sheared off her stern pulpit. It has been repaired, and she is now diligently remounting it. In addition to her seafaring abilities and evident shipboard resourcefulness, she is endowed with attractive feminine charms that are fully revealed by her bikini. To my way of thinking, there must be some way of using both her gifts and her talents to promote the boatyard repair industry in Bermuda.

1300 – We enjoy a leisurely and luxurious luncheon by the swimming pool at the Tucker's Point Club, graciously invited by Howard & Company. I savor a creamy pina colada with a smoked salmon sandwich. During our meal, we debate the appropriateness of feeding a visiting Labrador Retriever. Some maintain it is cruel to ignore his modest needs when we have so much on our table, while I expound the view that he is a salty dog experienced in the ways of wheedling excessive favors from naïve visitors. In other words, before we, especially Americans, become involved in unfamiliar overseas situations, we should take the time to learn the local culture and to know some of the countries' inhabitants.

1700 – What a stroke of luck. The Customs Office at St. George has cleared us out of Bermuda for departure tomorrow, so Garry does not have to go all the way to Hamilton during a taxi strike for a set of passport stamps. Common sense seems to have prevailed. One hearty cheer for the Government of Bermuda.

2000 – The whole crew meets Howard & Company at the Tavern-by-the-Sea for a farewell dinner. Tomorrow morning, we leave on our long, transatlantic journey to Ireland. I reflect upon this prospect with a mixture of emotions: gratitude for the opportunity for adventure, nervous anticipation of potentially dangerous situations, sadness at leaving my family for so long a time, and curiosity about how we will fare. Of this I am confident: the trip will seem entirely different when viewed after our arrival compared to before our departure.

2230 – I am too anxious to settle into my bunk yet. I cannot wait to get underway, yet I am held back by a slightly foreboding sense of danger and risk.

Reflecting back over 44 years, I relive my tension and excitement before my departure on my first transatlantic passage. In my unfading mental photograph, I see *Palawan* moored against the confining cliffs of Hamilton Harbor. Like myself, she and her crew are prepared, impatient to set sail, yet hesitant to get underway. Then, I faced one of my life's greatest experiences; my first voyage would mold many of my perceptions of life and change many of my attitudes forever. Never would I view life or the world the same way.

What will befall us on this voyage? Are there unknown dangers in the ocean, in our equipment, in ourselves? How will this passage differ from my previous one? Will it be smooth or tumultuous? What more will I learn?

It seems that our greatest achievements require us to leave our places of comfort and face failure by risking our faith in ourselves and our abilities. To learn and improve, we have to stretch ourselves. We must confront exceptional danger to achieve distinctive success. Once, I confided in Thomas J. Watson about a situation in which I found myself way out beyond the depth of my abilities. In reply, he smiled and said, "That's when you are learning."

Some think of sailing as a competitive sport, but it is much more than that. It is a way of life, a mentality that allows a person to meet the challenges of one of the earth's most ancient elements: the eternal sea around us. I feel its allure in the tides of my restless blood. The ocean calls.

PART II

Transatlantic Passage

St. George, Bermuda
to
Kinsale, Ireland

June 25th to July 14th, 2004

Friday, 25 June 2004 – Bermuda – Atlantic Ocean 1st Day

0745 – We cast off our mooring lines and get underway for the fuel dock, where we tie up to top off our tanks and fill the fuel jugs lashed on deck.

0830 – Howard and his companions arrive at the pier. Doris and her friend, Maryanne, comprise *Diva's* Departure Committee, giving us send-off encouragement—or perhaps just encouraging us to depart.

1125 – We cast off our docking lines for the last time on this side of the Atlantic. We are now officially underway for Ireland. On this part of our journey, we will not be racing against competitors; instead, we will be racing against time.

We must arrive in Ireland before the CCA cruise begins, and I must arrive in time to keep my travel arrangements and hotel reservations for my planned trip to Ireland and southwestern Scotland (to Cork, Dublin, Belfast, Ayr, Rothesay, Glasgow, and Edinburgh). I also intend to take an excursion on the world's only ocean-going, steam-powered paddle wheel vessel, the *Waverly*.

1150 – We clear the inner channel.
Wind: W (270 degrees) at S-78 knots.
Boat: C-094 degrees, S-5.5 knots.
Temperature: 91 degrees on deck, 85 degrees below decks.

We are sailing dead downwind, wing-on-wing, with the main to starboard and the genoa hauled out on the spinnaker pole to port. It is slow and hot. We rig the awning for some welcome relief in the shaded cockpit. This scene seems distressingly familiar.

Our first navigational waypoint in the Atlantic Ocean is designated *Point Able*, presently located at Latitude 40 north by Longitude 50 west. This is a navigational point in the North Atlantic at the southernmost point where icebergs are located and is strictly observed by vessels traveling both east and west. Thus, knowing its location is a critical safety measure (Illustration 35).

Several times a day, we receive ice reports generated jointly by the federal National Oceanography and Atmospheric Administration (NOAA) and the Canadian Coast Guard that are broadcast over Inmarsat in the form of charts displayed on our PC screen. They are comprehensive and accurate. This is a truly excellent and indispensable service. Neil is our official "weather expert" in charge of this vital function. He tries repeatedly to educate and guide Garry, our navigator. We earnestly hope for his success in meeting this challenge. Either way, like the passengers on the RMS Titanic, we will share their fate.

Thus, with NOAA's information, we determine Point Able's location. In fact, we have immense powers of discretion, even the option of changing its designation to *dis-able, un-able*, or even *dispic-able*.

Our course to Able-1 is 68 degrees, or ENE. We are now making 4.9 knots. By my calculations, we need to average 5.6 knots to arrive in Ireland, some 2,700 miles distant, in 20 days.

1230 – We are passed by two immense cruise ships in succession, one to starboard and then one to port, each about a mile away (Illustration 36). They are outward-bound from Bermuda. I wonder if the watch on the bridge even notices us out here. I doubt that we even appear on their radar screens. Perhaps a passenger glances from his or her 14th story stateroom balcony, notices our small sail, and wonders fleetingly about us. Does our triangular white sail resemble an iceberg?

At this hour, the passengers are probably sitting down to lunch in an immense restaurant, refreshing themselves after an exhausting morning of intensive shopping in St. George or Hamilton. I empathize with their hardship, since we had only to top off the fuel tanks, inspect the rigging, navigate out of the harbor, and hoist and trim the sails. Fortunately, many of the passengers are unaware that their floating hotel has gotten underway or even know that they are out on an ocean. Perhaps, when some of them return to port, a friend will ask about their cruise, stimulating a vague remembrance of having seen a rather pervasively blue expanse during their recent vacation. At the time, they were just not curious enough to ask what it was.

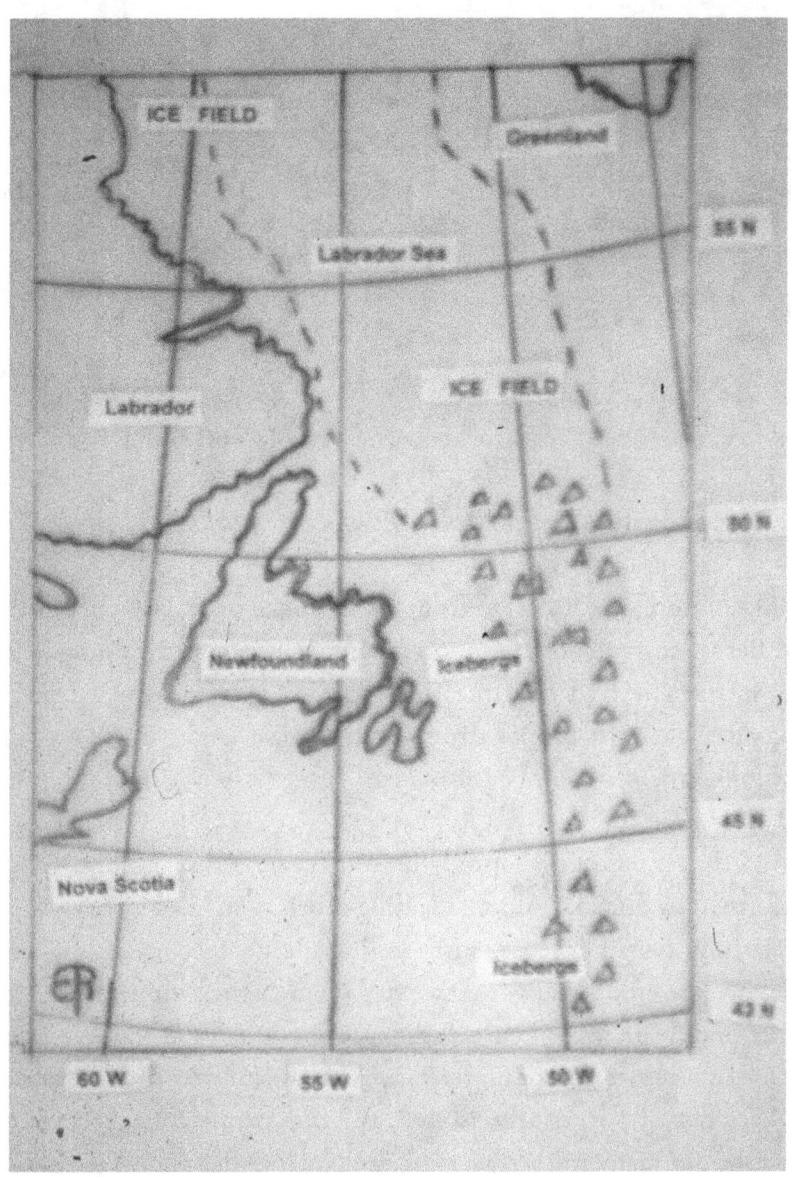

29. Point Able and Icebergs (Chart) (ER)

The sailing ship era is known as one of "wooden ships and iron men." Surely, ours will be known for its *iron ships and wooden men*. I wish the tourists all good luck on their daunting voyage. May their ship's rolling not stir their drinks too much.

30. Bermuda disappears Astern (ER)

1400 – We are now 10 miles from the entrance to St. George Harbor, and Bermuda gradually disappears from view astern, dropping below the horizon beyond our line of sight (LOS). Unless we make an unimaginable navigational error, this is the last land we will see for a very long time.

1430 – I play a CD, "Rhapsody in You," piano music composed and performed by our son, Alden. Hearing it brings my family back to me in a strong palpable sense, surrounding me perceptibly in our cozy boat. We are emotionally linked even when I am completely isolated in the middle of an immense, indifferent ocean. We are strongly connected in ways we do not understand, but of which we are fully aware.

Very few, if any, of us will have the opportunity to venture into space, but in many ways, traversing the North Atlantic in a small boat is a terrestrial experience which most closely resembles outer space travel. Aboard *Diva* we are surrounded by an unforgivingly hostile environment that will kill us very quickly if we make any serious mistakes or suffer any critical equipment failures. As a crew, we must have professional caliber operating skills gained through many years of extensive sailing experience. We must also meld all our efforts into flawlessly smooth teamwork.

Thus, in a sense, our ocean space shuttle, *Diva,* has left her launching pad in Bermuda and is commencing her great circle track, arcing northward toward Ireland. May God speed our voyage and may He "make the ocean its appointed limits keep," as the US Navy hymn so aptly phrases its prayerful appeal. Believe me, out here there is only one celestial power that can do that.

1700 – We have now sailed 28 miles since our departure.

>Wind: W (270 degrees), S-8–10 kts, occasionally gusting to 12 knots.
>Boat: C-075-degrees, S-5.5 knots. Wind slightly off our port quarter, still running wing-on-wing.
>Sea: Waves: 2-foot waves.
>Weather: Scattered clouds, otherwise clear.
>Navigation: Point Able bearing 69 degrees, distance 806 miles.

Our watch list has been revised:

	Bermuda	Transatlantic
A	Garry & Howard	Garry & Ernst
B	John & Neil	John & Howard
C	Rob & Ernst	Rob & Neil

1800 – Garry and I are now on watch. We experience occasional rolling and slatting, which does not make us happy. As Yogi Berra said, "Déjà vu, all over again."

We engage the autopilot, which I promptly rename "Otto-the-pilot." Welcome aboard, Otto.

1830 – I learn how to light the oven, with the assistance of Howard's surgical eye for operating detail and his encouraging directions.

1900 – We all feast on a sumptuous Italian dinner prepared by Garry and Howard, consisting of "many-cotti" (sic), of which some had "many" and others had at least a few. Unfortunately, no one receives a glass of Chianti wine, not even a single serving in a small plastic cup, in the preferred Italian manner. Our meal is completed by a refreshing, tropical Key Lime yogurt for dessert.

2000 – Our speed has dropped to 3.8 knots, so we roller furl the genoa, stow the pole, and turn on the engine, also known as "the iron jib." Our speed increases to 5.5 knots.

On my transatlantic passage on *Palawan* in 1960, I quickly learned that long distance, offshore sailing differs sharply from coastal racing or cruising. An ocean passage is an endurance contest between the crew and the boat on one side of the equation and the wind, waves, and weather on the other side. One aspect of this contest is a continuous battle to prevent excessive chafing to the rigging and sails. As the ocean swells swing the mast and the rigging, lines are constantly tightened and slackened against wear points and are soon cut through, while sails slap against rigging wear points and are rubbed apart.

As a result of this experience, I make a regular inspection tour from the cockpit forward, looking for any signs of chafing. I quickly find that the starboard mainsail preventer has become trapped under the lower block of the running backstay and shows evidence that it is being cut through at two points. In turn, this leads me to inspect the turnbuckle on the stays where the protective tapes have worn through, exposing the sharp ends of the turnbuckle cotter pins.

Garry comes forward to the mast with his tool kit and we spend about an hour performing turnbuckle surgery, twisting, cutting, and bending highly resistant stainless steel cotter pins until they are recessed within their turnbuckles. He does most of the work, while I supply a steady flow of appropriate tools—just like a hospital operating room. I wonder if *Diva's* health plan covers this. In any case, she certainly must be considered an outpatient, way out here in the North Atlantic.

Tomorrow, I will inspect the halyard situation and probably rig chafe preventers to hold them away from the mast. There is absolutely no substitute for vigilance. On the ocean, no one gets a second chance.

Even at night, the temperature below decks is 81 degrees, and the very high humidity makes it seem over 90 degrees. We open all the skylights and port holes for ventilation.

Saturday, 26 June 2004 – Atlantic Ocean 2nd Day

0300 – On watch. Powering with furled genoa to prevent slatting.
Position: Lat. N-33 degrees, 39 minutes, Long. W-62 degrees, 29 minutes.
Wind: Very light, virtually directionless
Boat: C-70 degrees, S-6.5 knots.

0430 – The eastern sky is starting to lighten, and by 0500 the stars have faded entirely, absorbed into the blue heavens.

0600 – We enjoy a soft, tropical dawn with small, puffy clouds scudding quickly along the horizon, their edges painted rose pink by the silently rising sun.

Wind: WSW (240 degrees) and has freshened to 10 knots.
Boat: Speed 6.8–7.4 knots, so we turn off the engine
Temperature: 79 degrees both on deck and below, very comfortable.

Over the last 12 hours, the wind has shifted from WNW (300 deg.) to WSW (240 deg.). Does this shift, along with the stratus clouds visible in the northeast, portend any changes in the weather?

0930 – It is becoming overcast.

1100 – Raining lightly now.

1200 – Noon.
Position: N-33 degrees, 39 minutes, W-62 degrees, 29 minutes.
Distance traveled: 134 miles
Distance to Go (DTG): 2,509 miles.

Wind: WSW, freshened to 10–15 knots.
Boat: C-70 degrees, S-7.8 knots
Weather: Overcast with rain.
Seas: 2–4 feet, WSW off our starboard quarter.

Our DTG is measured from our noon position to the Fastnet Light located off the southeastern tip of Ireland, from which we have about 47 miles farther to the entrance to Kinsale Bay and an additional 10 miles to the inner harbor.

For many centuries, celestial navigation was the only accurate offshore navigation technique available. Traditionally the navigator collected information at midday, determined the ship's position, and compared it to the previous day's noon fix in order to calculate the day's run over the last 24 hours. This was done at this hour because the navigator "shot the sun" with his sextant for a "noon sight," whereby he used the vertical angle of the sun above the southern horizon (when sailing in the northern hemisphere) to establish the ship's latitude. Eventually, the noon-to-noon regimen was termed a "ship's day."

To combine the ship's latitude and longitude, the navigator took a "celestial sight" at dawn and another at sunset, measuring the vertical angle of selected stars and planets. For the noon fix, the morning's sight was brought forward by a calculated distance in order to coincide with the noon sight. Then, the two sights were integrated to become "the noon fix."

Obviously, celestial navigation is possible only when the skies are clear enough to see the stars, moon, sun, and a sharply delineated horizon. Thus, a lapse of navigation during several days of fog can introduce substantial navigational errors. These errors become critical when approaching a dangerous shore while trying to make landfall at a harbor. As sailors say, if you "hit the bricks," you lose everything—and often, your life.

In our day of GPS "fixes," we still honor the celestial navigation tradition of calculating our day's run from noon to noon.

1215 – I can hardly believe it. More rain. Now it's raining heavily, a veritable orgy of atmospheric efflux. Why are we out here? Garry remarks,

"If this is what rich folks like to do, I'm going back to Brooklyn." I sense strongly that the entire crew will join him in New York City's sunny borough. Since the residents speak their own language stemming from Olde English pronounced with a Dutch accent, we will need a translator. The additional cost will be well worth it, just to get out of this rain.

I can think of few things more useless than rain on an ocean. What does it accomplish, aside from our acute discomfort? Does it water the floating seaweed? Does it rinse the raised backs of Portuguese man o' war jellyfish? To me, the rain would be much more productive over a desert. Is some unknown governmental bureaucracy in charge of this issue, as well?

1300 – The wind freshens unexpectedly and rapidly to 20–25 knots with tall, foaming waves about 15 feet high. We reef both the main and the genoa, our only prudent measure under these conditions. Our boat speed shoots up dramatically to 9–10 knots. Unfortunately, the blow seems to be temporary, lasting only an hour or so. Ocean swells have increased to five feet, and the boat rolls sharply whenever the wind diminishes. Our speed drops to 6.5 knots.

Today's ice chart shows icebergs scattered southeast of Newfoundland, located as far south as N-42 degrees at W-50 degrees, within only two degrees of our Point Able plot. Not much room for error, here.

1400 – On watch. Overcast sky. Wind is blustery but starting to diminish.

1430 – The weather is starting to clear. We unfurl the genoa and set it on the pole to starboard. Steering 70 degrees, dead downwind. We jibe and rig the genoa to port. Wind settles back to WSW (240 deg.) at 8–10 knots; our course is 70 degrees, speed 5.5 knots. Two conflicting sets of waves roll in, one from each quarter. A weather front, hurrying on its way through our small patch of the ocean, precipitates a brief period of rain followed by stronger winds.

1545 – My drawers break again. Aboard ship, this is considered *a severe breeches of etiquette.*

1830 – We are listening to Herbert Hildenberg, an amateur weather forecaster living in Eastern Canada. Every evening, as a personal hobby, he polls ships and yachts in the North Atlantic by radio telephone to obtain their current, detailed weather data. In return, he gives each of them an accurate, customized forecast for their location and projected track for the next three days. To prevent radio congestion and transmission interference, he assigns everyone a slot on his list and then calls out the vessels' names accordingly to initiate their reports. I estimate that he contacts approximately 20-30 vessels between 1800 and 2100 hours.

His forecast this evening for *Diva* is based upon the presence of a front just north of us, presenting us with options of sailing more northerly or more easterly.

(A) If we go north, we will encounter strong NW winds, shifting to NE or even E. This is not good, because we will be headed and will have to tack our way to windward, thereby reducing the rate of our progress considerably.

(B) If we continue east, we can expect predominantly SW winds of varying strength.

1900 – We partake of a delicious dinner of "chicken-catch-a-Tory" (sic), fresh salad and ice cream, all served in the comfortable "Cockpit Awning Café." Unfortunately, bar service is unavailable, depriving us of a good white wine, such as light, refreshing Chardonnay or perhaps even a Chablis, to complement our meal. Obviously, we should have ordered a bottle last night and placed it in the refrigerator for serving this evening.

In any case, the chicken may catch a Tory, but all we want is to catch some wind.

So far, the heat has been noticeably uncomfortable and discouraging. Within two days, I have thoroughly soaked three T-shirts with my perspiration. Consequently, I rotate their use, hanging them on the stern rail in the sun and the wind until they are merely damp before putting them on, unwashed, but half dry. Frankly, I find this situation thoroughly disgusting and unhygienic, but from a practical point of view, what else can I do?

1930 – I try to call Nancy, AKA Mariposa, in Newport, but am instead compelled to leave a message on the answering machine. I am not pleased at all. In life, I expect things to function reasonably well, and important things to function without fail. And Mariposa is supremely important to me.

31. In the Shade of *Diva's* Cockpit Awning (ER)
This is a very popular spot for gathering and socializing. I named it the Cockpit Awning Café, reminiscent of the *RMS Titanic's Café a la Carte*, which was very popular aboard that vessel.

Sunday, 27 June 2004 – Atlantic Ocean 3rd Day

Noon Report:
    Position: N-34 degrees, 45.7 min, W-60 degrees, 13.2 min.
    Distance: Last 24 hours, 130 miles
    DTG: 2,381 miles
    Wind: WNW (340 deg.), 15–18 knots.
    Boat: C-70 degrees, S-6.7 knots
    Weather: Cloudless, hot, and humid
    Seas: Breaking and thundering
    Temp: On deck 94 degrees, below 83 degrees.

0001 – I come on watch, furl the genoa, and start the engine. Boat C-77 degrees, S-6.5 knots. The temperature on deck is 76 degrees, comfortable enough to wear a T-shirt and shorts.

0200 – A half-moon lights up our sails as if it were a hazy day, rendering all the details of our rigging sharply visible. Almost imperceptibly, the moon gradually sets as a golden disk in the west.

As we sail northward from Bermuda, the atmosphere becomes noticeably mistier and the sky is softened by haze. This sky contrasts sharply with the evenings before our arrival in St. George, when the stars appeared so large and bright that our mast almost seemed in danger of scraping against them. Now, they glimmer weakly through the humid mist.

In a few days, we will pass over the *Titanic's* grave off Nova Scotia. We will then proceed further north and eastward, crossing the latitudes of icebound Labrador. We count on the Gulf Stream to keep our path clear of icebergs and growlers.

0900 – Come on deck to the glorious sight of our surging ahead.

> Wind: WSW (240 deg.), S-15 knots with gusts to 18 knots
> Boat: C-77 degrees, S-7.0 knots
> Sail: Genoa winged out to starboard
> DTG: 593 miles to Point Alpha.

Our weatherman Neil explains there are two successive low-pressure areas pursuing each other in tandem to the north of us. The first is centered at Lat. 60-N and Long. 50-W, heading NE. The second is just departing Florida and is now accelerating to 25 knots toward the NE as it leaves the surface friction zone of land. As a result, Neil forecasts that we should have generally SW winds of 10–15 knots, occasionally strengthening to 20–25 knots. Good news.

0930 – Another set of drawers breaks—this time in the galley, not under my bunk.

0945 – Not having caught anything on his trailing line to date, Rob has formed a Fishbait Advisory Committee (FAC), which unhesitatingly chooses the "yellow teeny bopper" lure. In the manner of young women, we hope that our youthful allure will "land a catch."

1000 – On watch. Garry, Rob, and I jibe to wing out to port. The wind is bearing 340 degrees at 15 knots, and our boat is at C-70 degrees and S-6.7 knots. It is a toasty day, with a temperature of 92 degrees on deck under the awning and 85 degrees below.

During our releasing of the after guy, we incur an unwanted wrap of the genoa around the headstay and have to sail briefly by the lee to unwrap it, thereby risking a sudden flying jibe.

1230 – Garry prepares the perfect mid-ocean luncheon: grilled cheese and tomato sandwiches with fruit yogurt for dessert, complemented by frosty lemonade.

I admit to suffering from a severe case of *galley-phobia*. Is my fear evidence of reincarnation? Consider the possibility that I may have been a Roman or Greek galley slave in a previous existence, thus explaining my present aversion to any activities taking place in the galley. Are we connected with former lives?

1300 – The wind is steady, directly from astern with seas 4–6 feet high that cause considerable rolling. We rig the awning, and everyone prefers to sit topside in the cockpit in spite of the fact that we have opened all hatches and portholes to generate cooling breezes below decks.

1400 – Off watch. I catch up on my log entries and shoot video recordings and still photographs.

1730 – A ship passes us off our starboard beam. She is hull down with only her superstructure and masts visible. Assuming a height-of-eye of eight feet when standing in our cockpit, I estimate her distance from us to be about 10 miles. Her superstructure aft together with her six masts stretching all the way forward indicates that she is a bulk carrier.

1840 – We contact Herb for a weather consultation, and he reports that there is a weather front close by us to the NE, on the other side of which the wind ranges from SE to NE. Because the wind remains predominantly SW on the south side of the front, we decide to favor an easterly course over tending to the north. Herb confirms that we are in an adverse current, a warm back eddy from the Gulf Stream. By tomorrow, we should start to work our way out of it and get a favorable current of 1–2 knots.

1905 - As a result of Herb's forecast, we change course substantially from 70 degrees to 88 degrees.

2015 - I enjoy another glorious shower and shampoo. Washing away all my disgusting sweat and gritty grime feels like scraping barnacles off a whale's back—or so I imagine.

2100 – On watch. Having jibed on the previous watch, we are now wing-on-wing with the pole rigged out to starboard C-85 degrees, S-8.5 knots, surging occasionally to 10.1 knots.

32. Ernst at the Helm of *Palawan-2* in the North Atlantic, 1960 (Anonymous)

Lightning is visible to the north, off the port beam. The bright flashes in the night reveal a line of clouds that probably marks the front previously described to us by Herb.

The wind increases from 10–15 knots to 10–18 knots and varies in direction between WSW (240 deg.) and SW (225 deg.). Otto-the-pilot is steering. I find that by modifying the desired course input by plus or minus five degrees, I can achieve noticeable increases in our tracking stability and boat speed. Sailing speed requires constant vigilance.

2345 – Raining. The wind is becoming increasingly variable.

2400 – Off watch. If compelled to state the truth, which I usually am by my insistent, vociferous conscience, I cannot say that I enjoy standing on deck being soaked by useless rain. Aboard *Palawan* we encountered quite a bit of it in the North Atlantic as we approached Scotland. I expect to repeat that experience.

Monday, 28 June 2004 – Atlantic Ocean 4th Day

Noon Report:
    Position: N-35 degrees 50.0 minutes, W-57 degrees 44.7 minutes.
    Barometer: 1025
    Distance: Last 24 hours 138 miles
        Total to date: 402 miles
        DTG: 2,247 miles
    Wind: N (000 deg.), S-5–10 knots
    Boat: C-70-degrees, S-6.7 knots
    Weather: Clear, sunny with scattered cumulus
    Sea: NW (345 deg.), 10–12 feet, smooth swells, no breakers
    Temp: On deck 74 degrees, below 79 degrees, water 81.7 degrees.
    Current: 1.4–1.7 knots against us.

0600 – On watch. Earlier last night, we passed through a front at 2400 with showers, wind gusts, and wind shifts. It was then calm until just before we came on deck. Now, the wind is NW (315 deg.), S-7 knots, our boat C-75 degrees, S-6.2 knots.

Before waking for my watch, I had a curious dream that Nancy was singing in a large choral group, probably the Collegiate Chorale, of which she is a member in New York. I tried to accompany them, but I could neither remember the lyrics nor sing the music on key. The other chorus members kept staring at me and asking, "What are you doing here?" That is an excellent question, considering where I am now. Is there a subconscious message here? Is Nancy a diva? She certainly is mine.

Perhaps this dream was prompted by my seeing, on my previous watch, the outline of an anvil-shaped thunderhead cloud during a lightning flash. Is my dream a *flash* of inspiration related to *Verdi's Anvil Chorus* from his opera *Il Trovatore*?

0630 – A ship, another bulk carrier, is sighted off our port beam. She is headed NE, undoubtedly destined for a northern European port. Perhaps Rotterdam. What could she be carrying? Iron ore from Brazil? Coffee from Colombia? Cocoa from Costa Rica? Guano from Guatemala? Marijuana from Mexico? *¡Feliz viaje!* Often, commerce connects our interests in powerful ways that we *readily* perceive and understand.

0915 – A shearwater glides silently past our stern and hovers over our wake, trying repeatedly to pick up our fishing lure without success. The bird's vain efforts lead me to reflect that, ironically, failure has saved him or her from a fatal catastrophe—but the bird will never know this.

Does failure occasionally save us from a greater disaster? How can this concept be reconciled with our culture that demands an unbroken chain of success? Do we sometimes learn more from failure, while success only confirms what we know beforehand?

When I graduated from the Hotchkiss School, which is arguably among the best preparatory schools in our nation, I entered Brown University where I was required to take an English Language Proficiency examination. I flunked! I was in a state of grievous shock. I could not comprehend how I had managed to fail after receiving a thorough and demanding instruction in English and literature at Hotchkiss. My scholastically impoverished circumstances so embarrassed me that I looked aside when entering the remedial English classes. Suddenly and unexpectedly, I was among the failures, the rejects, the "huddled masses, yearning to be free" of English language requirements.

I had, however, very good fortune in failure: my professor was especially inspiring, knowledgeable, energetic, demanding and rewarding. He transformed my task of writing English into an enjoyable skill, which, even now, challenges me constantly to achieve greater satisfaction through improvement.

My professor released a buried desire in me for excellence of expression and competence in communication. By this, I mean more than literary interpretation—I refer to the process of creating original concepts and communicating them accurately.

Thereafter, in each semester of my remaining years at Brown, I took an English writing course: creative, theatrical, analytical, argumentative, and everything in between. In my case, Brown quoted Hotchkiss: "moniti meliora sequamur."

When I became Executive Editor of the 1963 *Liber Brunensis* yearbook, I authored most of the articles, analyzed important academic and institutional developments, and interviewed principal campus leaders and thinkers. Four years after my initial failure, I achieved the satisfaction of seeing my written word become a small part of my college history. I had, as the Germans say, "Glück in Unglück," literally, "good luck in bad luck."

As much as anyone, I enjoy success—for example, our vanquishing *Pamir* on the way to Bermuda. I do recognize, however, that the rough road to ultimate success has surprising curves in it—or, as expressed above, good fortune in failure.

1000 – Garry reports that the southernmost ice limit has moved southward from N-42 degrees 50 minutes to N-41 degrees 50 minutes. Does *The Iceman Cometh?*

1130 – Garry calculates our Great Circle Route (GRC) as a series of compass courses for each longitude interval of 10 degrees, starting at 50.8 degrees and terminating at 84.5 degrees. Thus, initially we will head approximately NE, and as we approach Ireland, we will adjust our course periodically southward until we are headed almost due east. The calculated courses are True, not magnetic, so they have to be adjusted for variation in the earth's magnetic field and deviations or distortions created by the boat's own magnetic field.

Because the earth is a sphere, and has been so for quite some time, determining a great circle route is a navigational technique designed for plotting the shortest route between two points on a spherical surface. This cannot be done on a flat chart, such as a Mercator's Projection, because flat surfaces can only approximate the geometric surface of round objects and, even then, only with a considerable amount of distortion (Illustration 43).

Our computer program stretches a theoretical mathematical string, or line, across a mathematically defined globe's surface, stretching from our starting point to our destination. It then calculates the course between each longitudinal meridian's waypoint. In our case, Garry selects eleven intervals with twelve waypoints.

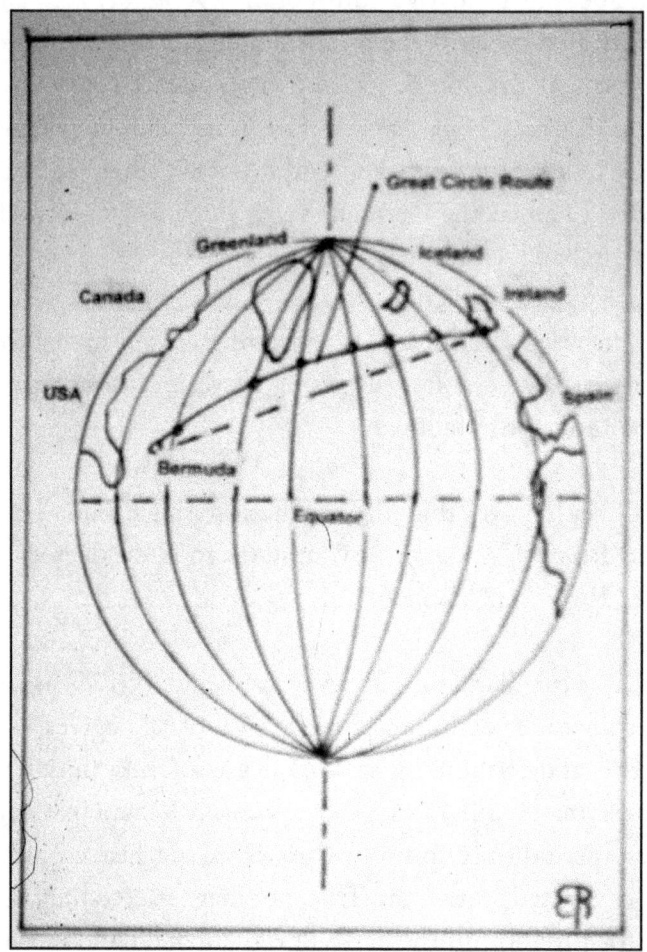

33. Great Circle Route (GCR) (ER)

1200 – Between occasional urgencies and emergencies, ocean sailing provides considerable time for reflection. As I mention in my Bermuda Race Log (Part I), sailing is understandably perceived by the general public as a "sport," but it is really much more than that. For those of us who know it well, we know it to be a way of life with its own distinctive mentality.

Manning a vessel, particularly a sailboat, requires individual skill of a high order, self-discipline when faced with known dangers, mature judgement concerning the correct courses of action when faced with unknown dangers, and the willingness to subordinate oneself as a team member to the common good. As the traditional maritime saying makes clear, a sailor has "one hand for the ship and one hand for himself." On the ocean we readily perceive and distinctly understand that we are all interconnected.

Our crowded living quarters require us to keep our individual spaces neat out of mutual respect for each other. We address one another with courtesy. Swearing is never heard, the sole exception being a traditional Rhode Island greeting favored by a particular crew member from that state.

The common language of sailing is unspoken. Everyone knows instinctively what he or she must do in any given circumstance and takes appropriate action immediately without being asked or suggested. Thus, if I am grinding on a winch, turning its handle in order to trim a sail, someone will assist me without saying a word. As a result, the two of us accomplish our joint goal of trimming the sail, which benefits the boat and therefore all of us.

If someone is washing dishes and I am not otherwise occupied, I assist by drying and putting them away. Together, we accomplish a task that is for everyone's wellbeing. Again, no one says a word, makes a request, or issues a command. Such instinctive teamwork is the essence of seasoned seamanship and survival on the ocean.

We are now a fully melded crew after five days to Bermuda plus four days across the Atlantic. *Diva* is a happy ship.

1700 – Our watch assignments are changed, as of 2100 hours:

Transatlantic-2
- A   Howard & Ernst
- B   John & Rob
- C   Garry & Neil

2000 – Becalmed, in the otherwise stormy Atlantic Ocean. We seem to be carrying our albatross from Bermuda with us. Did we snag one on Rob's fishing lure? Did he throw it back into the ocean secretly at night? So far, I have not noticed one hanging from anyone's neck.

Temperatures are comfortable at 76 degrees on deck and 83 degrees below.

2030 – I awake from a nap on the main cabin settee with a strange sense of abdominal tightening to discover John stepping on my stomach as he climbs out of his pilot berth above me.

2040 – I speak with my stepmother, Annelise, in Greenwich, Connecticut, using Howard's transoceanic cell phone. She seems surprised to hear from me. I guess most people are, most of the time. Understandably, she sounds deeply depressed over my father's death about three months ago. In addition to hearing her verbal expression, I sense her emotion as directly as palpable waves. I definitely sense a psychic connection beyond verbal expression, and beyond the constraints of physical distance.

She is undecided about going to *Tibberuphus,* our family home in Denmark, in July because of the unsettled weather there. Hopefully Ireland and Scotland, where I am headed, will have a different weather pattern.

Annelise agrees to call Nancy for me to tell her that we are all fine.

2100 – On watch. Becalmed. The wind is S, variable. Boat's C-70 degrees, S-6.0 knots. This evening is slightly cooler at 74 degrees, so I am wearing shorts and a medium-weight sweater.

I have a congenial chat with Howard about his son, who graduated from Stanford with a degree in theoretical mathematics. Now, *that* is intelligence of a high order. I guess that either you are endowed with such abilities or not. Perhaps I missed out, but there is no sense in worrying about it. I just have to do the best with the endowments I *do* have.

Tuesday, 29 June 2004 – Atlantic Ocean 5th Day

Noon Report:
    Position: N-37 degrees 2.7 minutes, W-55 degrees 21.4 minutes.
    Barometer: 1026
    Distance: Last 24 hours 136 miles
      Total to date: 538 miles
      DTG: 2,152 miles
    Wind: S (180 deg.), S-8–10 knots
    Boat: C-70 degrees, S-6.2 knots, on starboard reach
    Weather: Clear, sunny, scattered cumulus clouds on the horizon
    Sea: S (180 deg.), 1-foot waves, very smooth
    Temp: —
    Current: 0.3–1.2 knots against us

0600 – On watch. The morning skies are clear and the sea is calm. The wind is S (180 deg.), S-5 knots, boat's C-70 degrees, S-6.0 knots, and we are powering at 1,500 rpm. I am wearing only shorts and a T-shirt.

0615 – While at the helm, I look forward and notice that the genoa tack has become disconnected from the top of the furling drum and is hanging loosely from the forestay. Apparently, the recent slatting about has caused the shackle pin to work its way out of the shackle, which has fallen overboard, leaving the pin lying on top of the drum.

    Neil helps me correct this situation quickly by easing the genoa halyard, clipping in the replacement shackle and rehoisting the genoa.

0830 – The weather fax shows a strong low-pressure area with winds up to 45 knots, tracking NE from Cape Hatteras out to sea. Its track should make its closest point to us about 250 miles to the north. With some luck, we may be able to ride its winds, starting as S, then shifting to SW and finally to W. The barometric pressure reading is 1016 in the center of the low, while it is somewhat higher at 1026 for our location. This differential is not excessive, but it is enough to cause a moderate and steady airflow.

0920 – The wind is S (180 deg.) and strengthens to 10–12 knots, so we turn off the engine. Boat C-70 degrees, S-7.0 knots, which is respectable.

Diva is well equipped for short-handed sailing, having an autopilot, forestay furling for the genoa, slab furling for the mainsail, and an electrically powered winch on the cabin top. This versatile piece of equipment is employed for many functions: hoisting the main, trimming it, reefing it, and furling the genoa. It can also be rigged for trimming the genoa, if necessary. Through its mechanical assistance, this single winch replaces three crew members, effectively adding one person on each watch.

All other winches are self-tailing. Except for the genoa and spinnaker halyards, all lines lead to jamb cleats on the cabin top just forward of the cockpit, where they are easily handled and secured. On the whole, *Diva's* sail handling and trimming system is well thought out and very practical.

0930 – In one of our many conversations, I provide Howard with the useful information that Magellan's journalist, who chronicled his circumnavigation of the globe, was none other than Antonio Pigga Feta, spelled phonetically in Sanskrit (not to be confused with the French expression for striptease, *sans skirt*).

Life on a small boat in the middle of an ocean subjects a sailor to extended periods of boredom because, simply stated, all waves look pretty much alike. This situation forces some crew members to take refuge in their imaginations. So, in the distant realms of my consciousness, I experience a growing perception of Pigga's historic situation and an understanding of its relationship with our modern corporate culture in the United States.

As a recent graduate of the local Alphabetical Journalism Academy (AJA), Pigga Feta has been hired by his formidable uncle, Anuncio, the editor of the prestigious *Lisbon Bicoastal Daily Observer*, known locally by its acronym *Libido*.

Even though Pigga graduated last in his class at AJA, he does recognize the importance of competent writing for survival in the world of journalism and promptly hires his classmate Dagoberto, who graduated first in his class but cannot secure a job. The latter gratefully agrees to ghostwrite for Pigga for a 25 percent share of his salary.

Pigga becomes widely respected for establishing the political truism (certainly not altruism) of, "what counts is who you know rather than what you know." Pigga may be an incompetent journalist, but he is a wily entrepreneur who uses other people. Let's face facts: Pigga gets 75 percent of his salary and does no work, while Dagoberto receives 25 percent and does all of the work. If Pigga ever needs to look for other employment, he should seriously consider a position on Wall Street.

Unexpectedly, the *Libido* has been confronted with a threatening escalation of its production costs. Traditionally, it has been printed on inexpensive, locally harvested poppy-leaf pulp, but the public's recent discovery of the poppy's medicinal and self-entertainment properties has caused the leaves, their demand, and their prices to reach new *highs*. Consequently, the *Libido* has been forced to substitute expensive, imported paper. In response, Anuncio must cut staff expenses, starting with the only non-union member, his nephew.

Naturally, Pigga pleads for an opportunity to rescue his career. Anuncio relents, directing him to write a serialized article that is sufficiently compelling to raise the *Libido's* circulation enough to cover Pigga's salary. The editor informs him that two famous Portuguese mariners, Lorenzo and Fernando Magellan, have just arrived from Sevilla for a brief stopover, each in command of his own ship. Anuncio directs Pigga to chronicle the achievements of Lorenzo, a renowned water boat pilot, who has just devised a patented procedure for preventing rot in freshwater barrels by drilling holes in the bottom to let the water out. Lorenzo is in Lisbon to license his technology, and Anuncio is convinced that he will prove to be far more historically significant among venture capitalists than Fernando, who has the reputation of being a *dreamer* of ambitious expeditions that never result in immediate financial gains. Thus, Anuncio strictly instructs Pigga to ignore Fernando Magellan.

Pigga walks to the waterfront where both Magellans' ships are moored on opposite sides of the same dock. When refused permission to board, in his typical fashion, Pigga negotiates skillfully and deviously enough with the crew to secure an opportunity to hide himself aboard the ship—mistakenly, he finds himself on *Fernando's* ship. Later, when conducting his interview, the ship gets underway, and he accepts Fernando's generous invitation to accompany him around the world instead of being thrown overboard in a wine barrel, as a "talking message in a bottle." And, as they say, "The rest is history." Actually, it is Pigga's version of history.

Well, almost. During Pigga's extended absence, Dagoberto becomes Editor of the *Libido*. Upon Pigga's return, his book about his voyage sells so well that he buys the *Libido* and promptly takes a seventy-five percent cut out of Dagoberto's salary.

As Voltaire observed, "*Plus ça change, plus c'est la même.*" I would add, "Indeed, a bit like crossing a large ocean."

0945 – Out of a sense of inestimable indebtedness for this valuable information, I repay Howard by recounting a recent finding that the Scots probably discovered the New World, including America, before Columbus did. Subsequently, they instructed him on how to find it four hundred years after their original voyages to western lands, beyond Iceland and Greenland.

For several centuries, the Sinclair clan ruled northeastern Scotland and part of the west coast of Norway. Seafaring clansmen, they had sent many exploring and trading missions toward the west to Ireland, Iceland, Greenland, and Nova Scotia. As a result, the clan amassed substantial information on how to navigate to the New World, and they recorded it as both sailing directions and charts.

In the 1490s, a nephew of the clan chieftain committed a serious crime and was exiled for his personal safety to the Island of Madeira. Did he wear *broken drawers* instead of his kilt? In any case, during his stay in Madeira, he became acquainted with a visiting Italian mariner, Christopher Columbus.

Shortly thereafter, Christopher journeyed to Spain and secured venture capital from Isabella and Ferdinand for his expedition to open a new route to the Indies. Obviously, Christopher did not achieve this in the course of a casual conversation. Instead, he must have shown them a business plan. It appears obvious to me that in order to convince them of the soundness of his project, Christopher must have reduced the risk factor by presenting credible documentation that proved there was land where he was headed. I am convinced that Sinclair's nephew may have provided this vital information, thus ensuring the success of Christopher's exploratory efforts.

In this manner, the Scots discovered America, first on their own and then by helping Columbus find his "new world." Interestingly, Christopher, not the Scots, received the historical credit. Is there an unsettling lesson here about the importance of publicity and self-promotion? In any case, I am confident that Pigga would have received all the credit, had he been Columbus' confidant.

1000 – Off watch. We have so many drying clothes clipped to our rigging that I believe that our condition defines us as a "clipper ship."

1100 – Wind is piping up, so we furl the genoa and hoist the staysail, a perfect rig for a sunny afternoon sail in the mid-Atlantic.

1800 – On watch. An absolutely glorious afternoon sail with clear, sunny skies, and a comfortable temperature of 75 degrees. The wind is SSW (215 deg.) at S-12–15 knots with the boat C-80 degrees, S-7.5 knots.

1830 – We are listening to Herb's weather report. The dominant low that determines our conditions is now located SE of the Bay of Maine, at N-42 degrees, W-65 degrees, and projected to move to N-45 degrees, W-50 degrees tomorrow. His forecast for us is exceptionally favorable: SW winds at 10–15 knots for the next four days, through Saturday and possibly beyond. We could not have specified better sailing conditions.

1900 – Garry serves an unsurpassable dinner of eggplant parmigiana in the Cockpit Awning Café, accompanied by Ella Fitzgerald's music. *¿Todavia no hay vino, ni siquiera Chileno ni Argentino? ¿Que pasa?*

The wind increases pushing us along at 8 knots with surges to 10 knots. The evenings are becoming noticeably cooler, calling for a sweatshirt to supplement the usual T-shirt and shorts.

2100 – Off watch. Today's glorious sailing reminds me of the first part of my Atlantic crossing on *Palawan*. It is curious how the ocean is so variable from hour to hour and day to day, yet it is also so constant over the years and decades.

Wednesday, 30 June 2004 – Atlantic Ocean 6th Day

Noon Report:
   Position: N-38 degrees 29.2 minutes, W-52 degrees 27.9 minutes.
   Barometer: 1025
   Distance: Last 24 hours 162 miles
      Total to date: 700 miles
      DTG: 1,950 miles
   Wind: WSW (255 deg.), S-18–22 knots
   Boat: C-70 degrees, S-8.0 knots, dead downwind with one reef in the main
   Weather: Partly cloudy
   Sea: Steady swells, 10–12-foot waves with white caps
   Temp: 81 degrees
   Current: 0.2–0.6 knots against us

0001 – Today's first watch experiences a *foredeck fire drill*, a series of intensive sail changes. In succession, they put two reefs in the main, partially reef the genoa, take in the slatting forestaysail, shake out one reef in the main, and finally furl the genoa completely.

During the course of this activity, they break the self-tailing attachment on the genoa furling winch and then try to dismantle this infinitely complex mechanism in the dark. Such a task is difficult enough during daylight hours, and absolutely impossible at night. Let's just say that the winch won round one, decisively.

0300 – On watch. Light drizzle, blustery wind from dead astern. C-75, S-7.5 knots. We are carrying one reef in the main, and no genoa. *Diva* is riding comfortably in spite of her heavy rolling of 35–40 degrees. The dampness requires me to dress in full foul weather gear (FWG).

The wind drops occasionally, prompting Howard and me to wing the genoa to port without favorable results, so we refurl it.

0400 – I am watching for an opportunity to press on more canvas to drive *Diva* along more forcefully, but I have decided to wait until dawn. In my experience, the weather and wind tend to settle down in a more stable pattern just after dawn or after sunset. So, we will wait.

0415 – The horizon in the east is starting to lighten already at this early morning hour, proof of our northerly progress toward the realm of the *midnight sun*.

0600 – Off watch. I go below to fix breakfast. I have just poured several large glasses of grapefruit juice when the boat takes a particularly violent roll of 60 degrees down to her rail, thereby emptying all of the glasses down the front of my shirt. I find the galley's challenges exasperating before I have had even my first meal of the day.

Rob consoles me by relating that during his first business visit to the Soviet Union in the 1970s, the Russian hotel staff placed half a bottle of vodka at each place at the breakfast table. Fortunately, I did not spill vodka instead of fruit juice. Such a misfortune could never happen aboard *Diva* because she is a "dry boat," even in the bilges.

0815 – We rig the spinnaker pole to port, unfurl the genoa, and wing it to port. Otto-the-pilot now keeps the boat heading consistently and smoothly. Glad to have you with us, Otto.

0845 – We discuss the broken winch, and this leads to a discussion of the nubile "wench" on the boat alongside of us in Bermuda.

I relate to Rob and John an account of my first significant experience with women, which occurred at the age of twelve. It took place one sunny afternoon in a hayfield outside a village in Denmark. While the crew of a one-ring circus was erecting the tent, my friend Sven and I wandered about the premises. Suddenly, a young woman in rather tattered clothing chased us forcefully away, screaming in Danish, "Get the hell away from here, you stupid, wretched little bastards!"

I was both alarmed and deeply shocked by her negative attitude and her belligerence. Later, during the evening performance, I noticed a very attractive, smiling young woman selling candy to the audience. Only when she stopped directly in front of me did I recognize her as the young lady I had met previously. As Gilbert and Sullivan so aptly phrase such a realization in their operetta *The Sorcerer*, "Oh marvelous illusion…Oh terrible surprise!" Thus, at the tender age of twelve, was I introduced to the complex, and often inscrutable, nature of women.

1225 – We shake the reef out of the main, now C-70 degrees, S-8.3 knots. The wind is freshening to 20–30 knots from dead astern, and we are wing-on-wing with the pole to starboard. The seas are starting to build toward 15 feet and more, with their crests snarling with foam.

1300 – The wind gusts are diminishing.

1400 - On watch. C-80 degrees, S-8.0 knots.

1500 – The wind has dropped from 20–25 knots to 12–15 knots and is now veering to W (270 deg.).

1730 – Wind is falling rapidly now. We jibe to port, boat's C-70 degrees, S-7.2 knots.

1800 – Off watch. The wind has simply fallen apart. What happened to Herb's forecast for strong southwesterlies?

1930 – Wind is so light we are starting to slat.

2020 – Finally, we hoist our iron jib—or, as a landlubber would say, we turn on the engine.

Thursday, 1 July 2004 –
North Atlantic Ocean 7th Day

Noon Report:
    Position: N-39 degrees 38.0 minutes, W-49 degrees 31.7. minutes.
    Barometer: 1025
    Distance: Last 24 hours 154 miles
        Total to date: 854 miles
        DTG: 1,799 miles
    Wind: W (180 deg.), S-5 knots
    Boat: C-55 degrees, S-5.8 knots, motoring close hauled to port
    Weather: Stratus clouds, with a visible low-pressure area containing rain centered to the NE
    Sea: W swells, 3-foot waves
    Temp: 72 degrees.
    Current: 1.5 knots in our favor, giving us a COG-078, S-7.3 knots

We have now sailed about one third of our way to Europe. Since we are approximately 1,500 miles SSW of Greenland's southernmost tip and have just altered course significantly northward to NE (45 deg.), we have turned Point Able, transitioning from the Atlantic to the North Atlantic Ocean. From now on, we should be headed away from the icefields rather than toward them. Nonetheless, we must be vigilant for any rogue icebergs or growlers carried by the Labrador Current to unexpected locations.

0001 – On watch. Winds W (270 deg.), very light. It is strange how quickly weather conditions change. Yesterday, we had winds of 20 knots and waves of 12 feet with white caps, while today we have barely any wind at all.

Our base course is 75 degrees, but our actual course steered is C-45 degrees and S-4.0 knots. We are almost becalmed. We plan to work our way northward to search for more wind. The relative wind is off our port quarter, causing the genoa to collapse every time we head below 50 degrees.

0200 – Wind picking up slightly. Our boat speed is now a solid 5.5 knots with brief sprints to 6.7 knots. We are named, "the watch that went in search of wind."

I have a very convivial chat with Howard, a neurosurgeon who lives in Baltimore. He expresses his preference for New York City, where I live. Personally, I strive to avoid the appearance of parochial pride in my hometown, which sometimes is a controversial subject for people from elsewhere. New York is full of exceptionally interesting and diverse people who enrich my life, but although I enjoy the city wholeheartedly, I usually avoid talking about it.

On the other hand, I will readily express my strong opinion about the terrorist attack on the World Trade Center on September 11, 2001. I take the attack personally. Why shouldn't I? Nancy and I had two close friends who perished there. On that horribly tragic day, the entire world changed, not just the city of New York.

0300 – Boat C-80 degrees, S-7.5–9.0 knots, with a favorable current of 1.0 knot. We position ourselves about 2–3 miles from a band of low rain clouds in order to ride its local winds without being soaked. This is an act of delicate compromise requiring constant vigilance.

0730 – Garry prepares an unusually hearty breakfast of corned beef hash with fried eggs.

0755 – As I sit down, brimming with anticipation of a wonderful meal, I remark to John that our boat motion is comparatively docile, "like being at a mooring." At that precise moment, we heel abruptly over 60 degrees with our starboard deck instantly submerged. We are reeling in the midst of a flying jibe, caused by an overpowering gust of wind accompanied by a flood of flying water and rain.

I look up from the breakfast table to see the main boom's preventer wrapped tightly around the open hatch cover to the main cabin skylight. The aluminum framed window (cover) groans loudly as it repeatedly resists being ripped off and destroyed by the straining line. The rest of the crew rushes on to the rain-swept deck, clad only in their T-shirts and shorts, while I remain below, attempting to pry the preventer from its struggling victim. All the while, buckets of rain shower into the main cabin. Somehow, Howard and Rob appear above me on deck and together we loosen the outboard shackle, slacken the preventer, and release it from under the forward edge of the hatch cover. Finally, I am able to pull the hatch down to secure it.

I glance up at Howard and Rob, who are completely soaked by the rain and struggling on deck with flailing lines. For some unexpected and incomprehensible reason, I suddenly envision myself preparing to close the hatch on the conning tower of a submarine as we submerge in an emergency dive, abandoning both of them to drown in the empty ocean. My scene is imaginary, but so vivid it seems to be happening. How often did this situation actually occur aboard US, German, or Japanese submarines in World War II?

The abandoned submariners' emotions must have been indescribable, as they realized that they were being condemned to inescapable death. The remorse that haunted the survivors, assuming that the submarine was not sunk during the attack, must have been unforgiving. I am certain that the remaining crew members never outlived their feelings of guilt.

Why does the ocean appear to punish some with tragedy and spare others? As an example from history, the cruiser *USS Indianapolis* delivered the Fat Man atomic bomb to Tinian Island to be eventually dropped on Hiroshima by the B-29 *Enola Gay*. Shortly thereafter, the ship was torpedoed and lost 883 men out of a crew of 950. Most of the victims were devoured by sharks after the ship sank. Does this tempt one to believe in karma? If so, how can one account for the justice of such retribution if the captain and crew were only following military orders?

As for *Diva*, we are very fortunate that the hatch was not destroyed. I prefer not to imagine what it would be like to beat to windward in the tumultuous Irish Sea in winds of 45 knots amidst 30-foot breaking waves without our main skylight cover. No, thank you. I have already experienced these rough conditions aboard *Palawan* off the coast of Scotland.

I am intrigued. Why did I have such a sudden, vivid insight into others' experiences? Are all of us who travel upon the ocean connected by our mutual experience, both now and in the past?

0815 – We furl our jib, take one reef in the main, and clean up the mess of lines cluttering the deck and cockpit. On the whole, we handled the situation calmly without shouting or running about, which happens frequently on boats in emergencies.

As a result of this experience, Garry has concluded that we are too close to the weather front. Having sailed north to find wind and having found too much wind, we are now headed southward to find more manageable winds. As the Hotchkiss School motto admonishes, "moniti meliora sequamur," meaning, "having been warned, let us follow a better path." This is universally and eternally true, as sometimes we are reminded unexpectedly. For the moment, the crew aboard *Diva* is just trying to find any path that works.

At some point the weather situation must stabilize, hopefully in our favor. We have altered course drastically to 120 degrees ESE, when our desired course is 75 degrees ENE. Our speed is 6.0 knots. Beware of the long reach of the airborne *squallus nimbo cumulus*. The water temperature of 84 degrees indicates that we are still in the Gulf Stream, which is famed for its sudden squalls. Related to the subject of "better paths," we find the Gulf Stream is giving us favorable current of 2.0 knots.

It is now raining heavily. Well, at least our topsides are being washed down thoroughly. Our *Diva* is now *immaculata*.

1000 – On watch. We turn off the engine, unreeve the main, and set the genoa. We then set forth in search of our optimum course and boat speed in generally calm, dead downwind conditions. With the wind from due W (270 deg.), we set our initial broad reach course at 50 degrees, and the wind freshens enough to drive us at 4.2 knots, to which is added to about 1.2 knots of northeasterly current to a net over ground C-78 degrees, S-5.0 knots. This acceptable situation lasts about an hour, until the parade of thunderheads off our port quarter catches up with us and it starts to rain heavily. At this point, the wind drops below 4 knots. We spend our remaining three hours chasing boat speed at headings of 10–40 degrees. At times, the wind dies completely, leaving us without steerageway. Supremely frustrating.

During the downpours, I find that water runs up into my sleeves despite the fact that I do not raise my arms. This instance will be a good control test for my personally designed *sleeve stoppers* that I intend to wear during the next rainstorm.

1200 – John's noon position puts us at about one-third of the way to Ireland, about 850 out of 2,700 miles as measured to the Fastnet Light. We have achieved this distance in six days. At this rate, the remaining two-thirds should require about 12 days, including today, July 1st. Therefore, adding one day for a margin of error, I estimate that we could arrive in Kinsale as early as July 13th.

John announces we have traveled 15 degrees of latitude, placing us in a time zone farther to the east of Bermuda. We adjust our ship's clock and watches accordingly.

1300 – Raining exceptionally heavily, a veritable orgy of atmospheric efflux, stimulating my soaked imagination to search for relief in humor. I can imagine the advertising message as follows: the announcer asks, "Have you taken your Efflux today?" The crew answers in unison, "We have!"

1445 – A surprisingly sharp wind shift completely reverses the wind's direction from W (270 deg.) to E (90 deg.). Wind speed is now 8 knots.

Even a virtually perfect *Diva* can be improved in small, but significant ways. Today's variable winds confirm the need for wind measuring instruments for both true and relative wind directions and velocities.

1940 – We remove the second batten, which had broken, leaving a ragged edge that threatened to cut a hole in the mainsail. As a result, on certain points of sail and angles of sail trim, the main's leech flutters wildly. This wears the sail excessively. Thus, we have cured one problem and created another. To remedy the second problem, we take the slack out of the outboard reefing lines.

The above trade-off reminds us of a central concept in economics that nothing is free. Similarly, life often involves balancing incompatible alternatives.

2100 – On watch. Once again, we are the *wind-seekers' watch*. We are becalmed with periods of motoring interrupted with attempts to ghost along under sail. A huge, lingering weather front dumps a skyborne river of water upon us, accompanied by celestial drumrolls of cracking thunder and electrifying fireworks of lightning. It is an awesome performance of nature's raw power. In pagan times, it would have converted sinners into saints.

Outlined by the lightning flashes at night, I can see a line of squall clouds to starboard and most emphatically do not want to repeat this morning's wild breakfast ride. Not on my watch. As they say nowadays, "Been there, done that."

2300 – The wind is starting to fill in from the E (100 deg.). We tack to starboard, unfurl the genoa 50 percent, and wait for the wind—which is now gusting to 15 knots—to settle down.

2400 – I discover that my *sleeve stoppers* work very effectively during the torrential rain this evening, even though I am actively trimming sails, steering, and so forth.

34. North Atlantic Squall Line (ER)

Friday, 2 July 2004 – North Atlantic Ocean 8th Day

Noon Report:
    Position: N-39 degrees 32.7 minutes, W-47 degrees 36.0. minutes.
    Barometer: 1028
    Distance: Last 24 hours 69 miles
      Total to date: 933 miles
      DTG: 1,730 miles
    Wind: ESE (150 deg.), S-10–12 knots
    Sky: Overcast with localized thunderheads and rain
    Sea: SE, lumpy, 3-foot waves
    Current: Setting us to the north
    Boat: C-95 degrees tacking to C-160 degrees, S-7.0 knots
    S/trim: Tacking close hauled
    Temp: —
    Attire: T-shirt, shorts, and foul weather gear (FWG)

Yesterday's run is only 69 miles. As they said aboard the Armada in 1588, "Por el momento, nos parece que nunca llegaremos a Kinsale." We regret it, and I am sure they did, too.

0600 – On watch. No consistent wind. Again, we are the *wind-seeking watch*. Now on C-90 degrees, S-4.7 knots, motoring.

0700 – We tack SE in search of wind, unfurl the genoa, and finally settle on C-160 degrees, S-5.5 knots, which is directly away from Ireland. From everyone's facial expressions, I can tell the crew is skeptical about our navigation.

0800 – Garry announces that until further notice, we are to tack to windward in a band two miles wide, heading due east between the two latitude lines of N-39 degrees 32 minutes and N-39 degrees 30 minutes on a serrated track. We are able to head C-95 degrees on one tack and C-165 degrees on the other at a speed of S-7.0 knots on both. The situation is further complicated by the fact that we are also being set northward by a 1.2 knot current that is carrying us beyond the northern limit of our tacking band (see Illustration 47). Frankly, to me, it smacks a bit of round-the-buoy thinking, but this is just a difference of opinion—which often happens among experienced sailors. Such situations are always resolved in the Captain's favor, since his word is law.

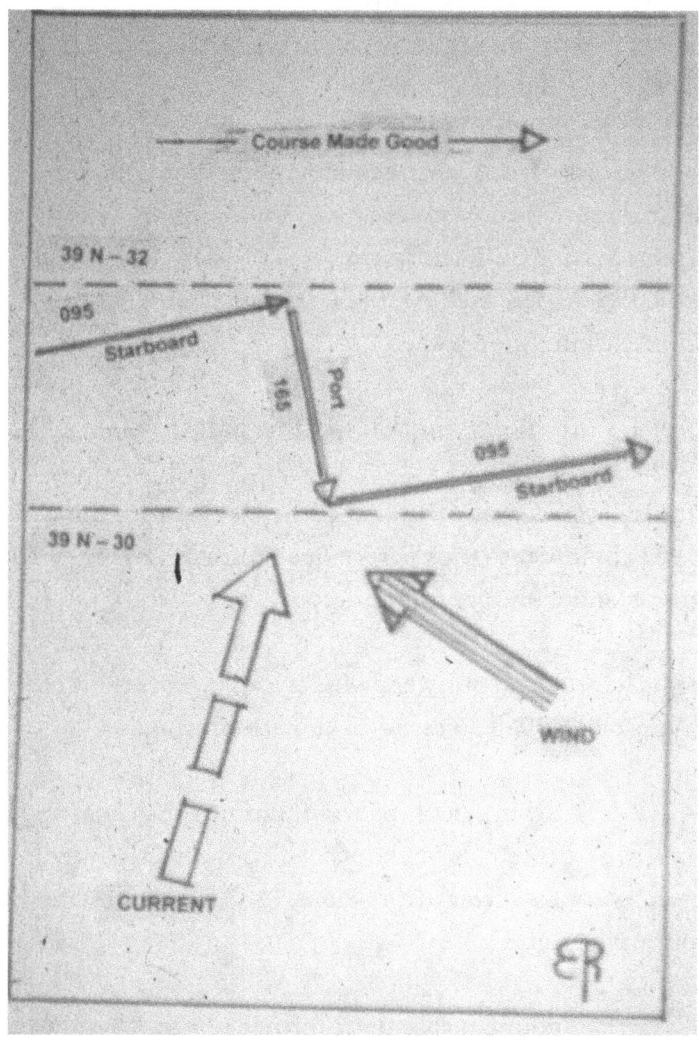

35. *Wind Seeking Technique*

1000 – I am grateful to be off watch. I no longer have to look at our discouraging compass headings. A small bulk carrier passes down our port side about two miles off.

Some dolphins come to play,
Around our bow,
But alas,
They do not stay.

A rhyme the not-so-ancient mariner, myself, composed more than a few leagues west of Tintern Abbey.

Most people confuse porpoises with dolphins. We use the term "porpoise" erroneously when we should identify them as dolphins. Popularly known as bottled-nosed dolphins, they are a cetacean mammal with a fish-like body and an elongated snout resembling a beak. In contrast, porpoises, which are also a cetacean, are 5–8 feet long, dorsally dark, and ventrally pale-colored, but have blunt, rounded snouts.

It is my understanding that dolphins are the shark's most feared enemy, because they will attack a shark as a group, ramming it repeatedly with their beaks until they draw blood. The other sharks in the vicinity are then attracted to their wounded comrade, whom they instinctively attack and devour, thus finishing the matter. This situation resembles that of Wall Street when a broker loses control of a large account. His associates instinctively help him sort matters out.

Thus, we humans share a common, vicious enemy with our seaborne friends. Everyone is excited by the dolphins' appearance and instinctively welcome them warmly as they surround our boat.

1130 – Although it was worth trying, we now give up our new wind-seeking technique. The entire crew is elated to see a steady course of 95 degrees blossom forth again on our compass rose. Once more, we are on a heading straight for Ireland. I feel very comfortable about this.

1430 – I take a nap in the forward cabin. A big mistake. I wake up to find myself floating in midair above the bunk because of our abrupt pitching. Overcome by strong feelings of nausea, I hurry aft into the main cabin where the boat's gyrations are less intense.

1730 – Suddenly, we hear shouts of "All hands on deck!" We have broken a line securing the topping lift to the boom, and it is flailing wildly about. We lower and furl all our sails and hoist Garry aloft on the mast, where he successfully retrieves the lost line.

1800 – On watch. It is raining and blowing, making this an uncomfortable watch. Wind is E (100 deg.), S-12–15 knots, the boat is C-65 degrees, S-6.0 knots. We have one reef in the main and the genoa is partially reefed with 70 percent of the sail out.

At the helm, I sit on the windward cockpit rail, close hauled on the starboard tack. I sail *Diva* like a dinghy, falling off slightly to power through the sloppy waves and heading up to 70–80 degrees in the puffs to claw our way to windward. In spite of the rain, it is thoroughly enjoyable at the helm to keep her both footing and pointing.

Like most boats, *Diva* handles well if canvased and trimmed correctly, but beating close hauled to windward is not her best point of sail. Instead, she must be sailed full without excessive heeling to overcome her substantial inertia.

2030 – I go below to enjoy a late dinner of a cup of tea followed by two seasick pills for dessert.

2100 – Off watch. I decide to camp out on a settee in the main cabin. As I sink slowly into comforting sleep, I recall images of a similar experience with soaking, stormy weather off the Scottish coast aboard *Palawan*.

36. *Palawan-2* Storming to Windward off Scotland's Coast, 1960 (ER)

37. Thomas J. Watson, Jr., on *Palawan-2's* Helm in the North Atlantic (ER)

Saturday, 3 July 2004 –
North Atlantic Ocean 9th Day

Noon Report:
    Position: N-39 degrees 52.7 minutes, W-47 degrees 56.0. minutes.
    Barometer: 1027
    Distance: Last 24 hours 67 miles
        Total to date: 1,000 miles
        DTG: 1,663 miles
    Wind: SE (135 deg.), S-13–40 knots
    Sky: Low overcast, raining
    Sea: SE, rough, waves breaking 10–12 feet
    Current: 1.5 knots, to the north
    Boat: C-60 degrees, S-7.0 knots
    S/trim: Close hauled on starboard tack with two reefs in the main and the genoa furled to 20 percent out, running backstays rigged.
    Temp: —
    Attire: T-shirt, sweatshirt, shorts, and foul weather gear (FWG)

I used to believe it was impossible to do worse than yesterday's 24-hour run of 69 miles, but we manage to beat that record. Today's run is a paltry 67 miles. To quote my good friends from Brooklyn, "Go figure." Well, I did: our DTG of 1663 miles at 67 miles/day equals 24.8 days remaining, plus eight days to date, for a total voyage of 33 days.

0300 – On watch. We finally find wind, and then some. Wind is SE (135 deg.), S-35 knots, gusting to 40 knots. Now *that's* a breeze. We take two reefs in the main, furl the genoa 80 percent and rig the running backstay to steady the mast's movements. The seas are initially 5–8 feet and build rapidly to 10–12 feet with large rolling whitecaps. Raining moderately.

Boat C-60 degrees, S-7.0 knots, close hauled on the starboard tack. *Diva* is riding comfortably, footing well, and heading reasonably close to our desired course. Otto is steering quite well.

0600 – Off watch. Below decks, the waves resound loudly, sounding as if someone is pounding on the hull with a sledgehammer. The cabin jumps about like a cocktail shaker, making all movement and all simple tasks extraordinarily difficult. Just putting on one's FWG takes twenty minutes.

0700 – I sleep unusually soundly until 1300 hours on the windward settee in the main cabin. I have a very vivid and alarming dream.

I am standing in the doorway to an unfurnished room with white walls. It is unusually cold, to the point where my breath is frosting. The room is dark except for a single bright lamp in the foreground. Its sharp light is mysteriously unable to illuminate the space beyond its immediately surrounding vicinity. I sense very strongly that I am viewing this scene in real time through someone else's eyes and realize intuitively that I am in a region of Hell.

If residence in this room in the afterlife is a sentence for sinning, I can only recommend to everyone in this life, "Behave yourself."

As I mentioned earlier, life on a small boat in the middle of an ocean subjects a sailor to extended periods of boredom because, simply stated, all waves look pretty much alike. This situation encourages some crew members to explore their imaginations, while others contemplate philosophical issues, including the nature of perceived reality and some of its hidden aspects.

Thus, I consider the nature of sleep, an important daily activity—or rather, a non-activity. I find it curious that we humans interrupt our daily pace and assume an insensate, dormant state for about seven hours per day. Personally, I have always assumed that a period of sleep is required to refresh the strength of our body, especially those parts that are particularly vulnerable to short-term fatigue, such as our muscles and eyes. Perhaps, however, our bodies have been designed and constituted in such a manner that they could support a moderate activity load for a continuous 24-hour period. Thus, under these conditions, we might need only brief periods of physical rest during which we would remain conscious, thus dispensing with longer periods of unconsciousness.

If the above option is possible, does it not suggest that our need for sleep actually serves some purpose beyond physical rest and repair? Could it be a period for rendering our minds open to other channels of communication? Communication with whom, and about what? Some possibilities include: our subconscious, our source of creativity, the "collective unconscious" as described by Jung, and even mysterious sources of premonition. What is the medium of this communication? Most likely dreams.

Consider a recorded instance of a most curious and alarming dream that occurred to President Abraham Lincoln on the evening of Thursday, April 13th, 1865. He dreamt that he awoke to find the White House in an unnatural state of stillness, wandered downstairs in his nightshirt to find the cause, entered the East Room, and found a hushed crowd filing by a coffin draped in black velvet. When Lincoln asked one of the guards about who was dead in the White House, the soldier replied, looking through Lincoln as if he did not exist, that the President had been killed by an assassin. At that instant, a woman in the dream shrieked and Lincoln woke up, suffused in sweat.

Abraham Lincoln was assassinated on the following evening of April 14th, Good Friday.

0930 – We tack again to C-220 degrees, west of south, in search of better weather, more favorable currents, and southwesterly breezes. Personally, I think we are chasing a unicorn. No one has caught one yet.

To some degree, I am an old-fashioned sailor and believe that navigating a deep-water passage is really a balance between one's desired heading and the boat's speed. In short, one simply steers the closest course to the base course (GCR) and then sets and trims one's sails to maximize boat speed. In terms of anticipated winds, under certain circumstances it might be advantageous to favor one side of the rhumb line. To my way of thinking, when your boat speed averages 6 knots, it makes little sense to chase weather fronts or barometric pressure zones that are passing at 20–30 knots across the ocean.

My viewpoint: just take the weather as it comes and sail the best you can.

1400 – On watch. Wind SE (135 deg.), S-5–10 knots, boat C-80 degrees, S-8.0 knots, under full sail on a close reach to starboard. Overcast and raining. By now, because of the humid weather for the last several days, everything below decks has become damp, rendering the term "dry" a relative one.

Neil, John, Rob, and I engage in a long discussion analyzing our predicted arrival in Ireland. With a DTG of 1,000 miles, at an estimated distance/day of 140 miles, we will need 12 days. If we include today in the time required, we should arrive on July 14th or 15th.

1840 – In an effort to remedy the pervasive dampness below decks, we turn on the forced hot air cabin heater and the temperature immediately soars from 73 degrees to 78 degrees. Toasty, warm, and dry.

1900 – Neil serves a sumptuous "veal piccadillo" (sic) with hot, home-baked cherry pie for dessert. I believe that traditionally one serves white, not red, wine with veal.

Sunday, 4 July 2004 – North Atlantic Ocean 10th Day

Noon Report:
    Position: N-41 degrees 00.0 minutes, W-43 degrees 21.0. minutes.
    Barometer: 1027
    Distance: Last 24 hours 147 miles
        Total to date: 1,147 miles
        DTG: 1,521 miles
    Wind: SSE (165 deg.), S-15 knots and building
    Sky: Overcast, stratocumulus
    Sea: SE, slightly lumpy, 4–5 feet, leftover from yesterday
    Current: 0.5 knots, against us
    Boat: C-110-degrees, S-7.8 knots
    S/trim: Close reach on starboard tack
    Temp: —
    Attire: T-shirt, shorts, and foul weather gear (FWG)

In honor of July 4th, our 24-hour run shot up from 67 miles to a respectable 147 miles. This is also my son, Ernst Jr.'s, birthday.

0001 – On watch. We spend three hours passing through a weather front. Wind is SE (135 deg.), S-5–15 knots, boat C-080, S-5.5 knots, sea is 3–5 feet. The rain varies from moderate to intense tropical downpours. We are keeping our course as the wind maintains its direction, increasing in strength every time we pass under dark squall clouds. We have learned from our previous knock blow during breakfast and are now extra vigilant, standing ready to furl the genoa quickly and release the main sheet in case we are hit by a rogue gust of powerful wind reaching out from under a cloud. We have learned to keep a very wary eye to windward on the treacherous *stratus nimbo cumulus*.

0830 – Garry and John prepare a festive Fourth of July *Omelette a la Diva, de la 4me etage,* translated roughly as: an omelet raised to the fourth power. This is served with a freshly baked three-layer cake. Considering the fourth power and the three layers, today's program turns out to be quite mathematical, but we are convinced that in the end that it all adds up. And certainly, it adds to our morale.

0945 – In order to reduce the hazard of slipping on the cabin floor, I clean boards of our body oil, which has been deposited by our bare feet as we walk about.

1000 – On watch. Wind, SW (135 deg.), S-12–15 knots building to 15–18 knots. Boat C-110-deg., S-7.8 knots. We are headed slightly east of our rhumb line course in order to skirt along the southern edge of a deep low-pressure area to the north that has gale force winds of 35–40 knots. This is a good example of a situation where it makes sense to adjust one's course moderately to avoid a clearly identified weather hazard.

Fastnet Rock, our intended landfall off the southwest tip of Ireland, now bears 71 degrees. Our course over ground (COG) is 95 degrees, which means we are about 25 degrees low of our rhumb line course.

1040 – We commence transferring 55 liters (15 gallons) of diesel fuel from our reserve canisters on deck to our main tank below the cabin floorboards. This takes about an hour of hand pumping the fuel through a long hose stretching from the fantail, across the cockpit, down the main hatch, past the galley and the navigator's station, into the main cabin bilge.

1200 – Because today is my eldest son, Ernst's, birthday, Garry very kindly allows me to send a greeting to him in Copenhagen, Denmark, using the ship's PC wireless email service:

"Happy Birthday to you and your country
from the North Atlantic Lat. 41 north, Long. 43 west.
Much love, Dad"

I clearly recall the day of Ernst Jr.'s birth. Because New York Hospital was virtually empty for the holiday weekend, the obstetrician invited me into the operating room to stand at his elbow during the delivery in order to witness Ernst's arrival. This happened long before the presently popular (and correctly so) participation of husbands in support of their wives during their child's birth.

To witness Ernst's birth, I donned a green operating room uniform. The entry into this world of a living person who did not appear to exist until the present moment can only be described as, "a miracle of God." There was a palpable supernatural presence in that mundane operating room. I know this to be true because I actually felt it. Only upon later reflection did I realize the significance and identity of the spirit of creation.

Later that evening, Ernst lay wrapped in a blanket in his hospital bassinet. As I was looking at him, he winced gently every time he heard the distant, muffled fireworks explode, celebrating his birth. Considering his auspicious arrival, Ernst has been surprisingly modest in his self-opinion since then.

In contrast, Lord John Patrick Creighton-Stuart, who rebuilt Mount Stuart Castle on the Scottish island of Bute, had the entire ceiling of the bedroom where he was conceived painted with an extensive celestial scene depicting the positions of the heavenly orbs at his moment of conception.

I believe that New York Hospital's bureaucracy would not be favorably disposed to consider a request from me for a similar decoration, not even if I personally painted the operating room ceiling. Perhaps, I should adopt the name of my Italian friend Michelangelo Buonarotti by signing it as, "Buona Rota" or even "Buona Rothe." Unfortunately, he was unavailable, being out of town on an assignment with the Vatican.

1345 – We come to magnetic course 83 degrees which yields a COG of 71 degrees, directly toward Fastnet Rock some 1,500 miles away. We are on a broad reach to starboard doing 7.2 knots, and the boat rolls noticeably more. Wind is 20 knots, with white caps strewn across the ocean. Several large patches of blue sky expand off the starboard beam. The boat is starting to dry out a bit as we open hatches, skylights, and portholes for fresh air welcomed below.

1400 – Off watch. I contribute to the July 4th celebration and to the welfare, hygiene, morale, and morality of the crew by shaving, brushing my teeth, applying deodorant, and changing my shirt. My first shirt has lasted for the first nine days of our voyage. It has served me well. I also have donned a fresh pair of slacks. *Moniti meliora sequamur*. Indeed, I have done just that.

1600 – Garry starts to prepare our special July 4th dinner. Howard has baked a cake and I assist with lighting the oven. It strikes me as a bit strange that a national holiday should seem significant when we are totally isolated from shorebound concerns, on a small boat in the middle of an immense ocean. Such an occasion, however, seems almost *more* significant to us, probably because in our isolation it becomes our link with our home life. So, we celebrate with special enthusiasm.

1830 – I call Nancy, AKA *Mariposa*, on Howard's global cell phone. Somehow, she sounds subdued, even a bit depressed. This is not the first instance my call has this effect on her. She is fine, as are Whit and Alden. The bathroom renovation in our New York apartment has turned out well.

I am very grateful that earlier today, she tried to call Ernst Jr. in Denmark to wish him Happy Birthday. That gesture typifies Nancy's kind consideration for others.

This evening our special friends, Isabel and Rob Walker, have invited her to join them at NYYC Harbor Court for dinner. Special fireworks are planned to celebrate the port call of the new, magnificent, super ocean liner, *Queen Mary-2 (QM-2)*. Apparently, she is visiting Newport because her safety from terrorists could not be guaranteed in New York Harbor.

It appears that Osama Bin Laden and Al Qaeda continue to impact our lives long after 9/11, 2001.

1930 – After three hours of arduous preparation, Garry serves a spectacular July 4th dinner of *Veal Picante a la Divante* accompanied by mashed potatoes and a freshly baked layered pound cake with bitter chocolate frosting. He has achieved a culinary tour de force. Perhaps this will be recorded as our galley's high-water mark. Champagne, anyone?

Everyone greatly appreciates that Garry has considered our culinary requirements so carefully. They are key to maintaining shipboard morale and rendering our voyage an enjoyable experience.

In the middle of this amazing repast, the wind stiffens suddenly and significantly, so we break off our celebrations briefly to double reef the main, hoist the staysail, and furl the genoa.

2100 – On watch. Wind SE (135 deg.), S-10–12 knots, boat C-104 degrees, S-5.7 knots, sailing on a close reach to starboard. Very lumpy seas make *Diva* roll markedly. Our weather forecasting friend, Herbert, predicts some very strong SW winds of 25–30 knots in our area, so we reduce our canvas to a minimum of a double reefed main and only the staysail as a prudent precaution. Garry is a wise sailor who does not place us at the mercy of the unmerciful elements.

2400 – Off watch. I decide tentatively that this logbook's title is to be *Ocean's Call*, alluding to John Masefield's poem *Sea Fever*, which expresses the ocean's eternal, instinctual attraction. The explanatory subtitle will be "A Transatlantic Passage," an adventure that many sailors, and perhaps even some non-sailors, would like to experience.

We are presently about 1,200 miles due south of the southernmost tip of Greenland. Imagining the magnificence of this icebound area stirs the incipient desire within me to see it. Perhaps another adventure, in another time? *The eternal ocean's call.*

Monday, 5 July 2004 – North Atlantic Ocean 11th Day

Noon Report:
    Position: N-41 degrees 43.0 minutes, W-40 degrees 19.0. min.
    Barometer: 1027
    Distance: Last 24 hours 151 miles
       Total to date: 1,298 miles
       DTG: 1,384 miles
    Wind: SW (225-deg.), S-30 knots with higher gusts
    Sky: Clear with scattered cumulus
    Sea: W, 10–15 feet, with mountains of water rising up on the horizon and thunderous white caps foaming everywhere.
    Current: 0.8 knots, against us
    Boat: C-70 degrees, S-8.3 knots, surging to 9.0 knots
    S/trim: Broad reach on starboard tack
    Temp: —
    Attire: T-shirt, long pants, and FWG

0600 – On watch. Wind is SW (225 deg.), S-20–25 knots and building. The sea is awash with white caps. The next three hours place many demands upon our sailing skills but also reward us with well-earned satisfaction. We are carrying two reefs in the main, a staysail, and a partially furled genoa. When we surge to 9.1 knots, our steering becomes labored, so we furl the genoa farther back to only 20 percent out.

0800 – We change course to 70 degrees, S-8.2 knots, to a broad reach on starboard tack. We unfurl the genoa slightly from 20 percent to 35 percent out. We carry the sheets slightly snugged in to flatten the genoa in order to push our bow to leeward if *Diva* should attempt to round up out of control.

0840 – Furl the genoa from 35 percent to 20 percent out. We disengage Otto-the-pilot and steer manually after he almost jibes the boat. Winds are now 35 knots. The sea around us appears to be white foam rather than blue ocean.

Today we experience the exhilaration of driving our diminutive clipper ship at a thundering speed through the trade winds under sunny skies, with comfortable temperatures, powerful winds, and seas foaming with white caps on all points of the compass across the horizon. Through the lens of shared experience upon the eternal sea, I sense that I have stepped back into the 1850s clipper era of *wooden ships and iron men*. *Diva* has become our time machine, our intrepid time-and-spaceship, navigating the realms of relativity across the constellation of time.

Like a wave breaking upon a beach, a vivid memory surges back to me. Several years ago, when I was an eleven-year-old student at the Greenwich Country Day School in Greenwich, Connecticut, curiosity compelled me to wander into the mystic section of the school library reserved for upper school students in search of enlightenment. There, on a high shelf, I found a massive book, titled *The Log of the 'Cutty Sark.'* It referred to the famous English "wool clipper" that transported wool from Australia to England during the 1870s. Immediately, I recognized that her story was not *shear nonsense*. As proof of this, the *Cutty Sark* can be seen today in the drydock at the Maritime Museum in Greenwich, England, about fifteen miles downstream from the Tower of London.

I read the book with a sense of adventure and learning. It contained a striking photograph of one of *Cutty Sark's* captains roller skating around the heaving afterdeck in mid-ocean. If he had been of religious bent, he would have been considered *a holy roller*. This is most likely not the case, however, since at sea it is deemed strictly inappropriate to maintain a holier-than-thou attitude. On the other hand, maintaining a *rollier-than-thou* stance is quite understandable, especially if you are becalmed en route to Bermuda.

Apparently, many clipper ships were so narrow in the beam and their lines so refined for speed that they would not float upright without the weight of some cargo or ballast in their holds. This deficiency was remedied by a special loading procedure: as inbound cargo was offloaded from one part of the hold, outward-bound cargo was simultaneously loaded aboard into another. Thus, the ship was maintained properly ballasted while alongside the pier. The book contained a photograph of a capsized clipper ship alongside a dock. The vessel was lying on its side with its multitude of yardarms poking through the roof of the warehouse. I could clearly read the dockside observers' minds: "moniti, meliora, sequamur," or in other words, "There must be a better way to offload a ship."

1330 – 1430 – We set the ship's clock and our watches one hour ahead to the next time zone farther east.

1800 – On watch with John, according to our revised watch list:

Transatlantic-3
A   John & Ernst
B   Garry & Rob
C   Neil & Howard

Sometime between 1800 hours and 1900 hours, we pass our halfway point, calculated as follows: 2,644 miles—St. George to Fastnet, plus 46 miles – Fastnet to Kinsale, totals 2.690 miles, yielding a halfway distance of 1,345 miles, which is equivalent to two Bermuda races.

Arriving at turning points in a long voyage often inspires reflection. We find ourselves on an ocean that is immense and primeval. It is the earth's single largest feature, covering two-thirds of its surface and virtually governing its weather. The ocean became the earth's dominant element when the molten ball of rock cooled, and since then it has witnessed every continent created—of which many have appeared, drifted across the earth's surface, and then disappeared into the molten lower regions of our planet.

The ocean is indifferent to our fate and our pretensions. It does not care about anyone's gender, race, religion, or even whether or not one has *broken drawers*. The sea is not impressed by anyone's intelligence, wealth, professional expertise, geometry exam grades, or club memberships.

Anyone who traverses the ocean's surface does so only with its permission, which it grants temporarily by suspending its destructive fury. Egotists who fail to respect its limitless power are eventually consumed by their misplaced pride, as they commit a fatal error—usually small at the outset—that starts a chain of deadly events. The sea waits patiently for its opportunity, then swallows all fools without leaving a trace on its surface.

I refer any skeptics on this matter to Captain Ahab of the *Pequot*, Captain Smith of the *Titanic*, and Captain Turner of the *Lusitania*. For the committed skeptics, a conversation with Vice Admiral Chuichi Nagumo aboard the Japanese carrier *Akagi* during the Battle of Midway would be most instructive. As Commander-in-Chief of the First Air Fleet, he managed to lose four of Japan's largest fleet aircraft carriers—the *Akagi*, the *Hiryu*, the *Kaga*, and the *Soryu*—on a single afternoon. It is true that weapons were the source of the ships' destruction, but once wounded, the ships were quickly consumed by the sea. On the ocean, matters can go terribly wrong terribly quickly.

According to Commander Masataka Chihaya's post-battle analysis, it was a widely held belief in the Japanese Navy Command that the Midway disaster was visited upon their nation *as punishment for its excessive conceit*.

Some mariners, such as Herman Melville, have compared the ocean to the face of Fate or even to that of the Divine Creator.

As our little cosmic voyager crosses the hostile expanse of the high seas, I prefer a more hopeful view expressed by Brown University's motto, "In Deo Speramus," or, "in God we hope." Indeed, we do.

1930 – Suddenly we hear shouts, "All hands on deck!" and the crew scrambles topside. The topping lift has chafed through again and is swinging about the mast. We hoist Garry aloft and he deftly retrieves it.

2000 – A large black bulk carrier headed for Europe passes us on our starboard side.

2055 – As I am about to enter the companionway to go below and off watch, a wave slams into the boat, causing me to lose my balance. I lose my grip and fall some two meters (six feet) from the hatchway down against the leeward cockpit coaming, landing directly on the ribs of my lower right back.

I consider myself very fortunate not to have suffered a broken rib or perhaps even a broken back. How incredibly horrible paralysis would be. This confirms to me how we are always vulnerable to incapacitation.

Tuesday, 6 July 2004 –

North Atlantic Ocean 12th Day

Noon Report:
    Position: N-43 degrees 14.0-minutes, W-37-degrees 18.0. minutes.
    Barometer: 1026
    Distance: Last 23* hours 147 miles *(reset ship's clock)
        Total to date: 1,445 miles
        DTG: 1,223 miles
    Wind: SSW (205 deg.), S-15 knots
    Sky: Clear with scattered cumulus
    Sea: SW, 10–15 feet, slightly lumpy
    Current: 0.2 knots, against us
    Boat: C-70 degrees, S-8.0 knots
    S/trim: Broad reach on starboard tack
    Temp: —
    Attire: —

0300 – On watch. The wind is generally southwest and appears to be holding. Wind is SSW (205 deg.), S-15 knots and the boat C-70 degrees, S-7.8 knots. After dawn, the wind pipes up a bit, we unfurl the genoa from 70 percent to 100 percent, and our speed increases to 8.0 knots. This small speed adjustment may not seem like much, but it adds about five miles to our daily run and amounts to a 100-mile gain during a 20 day passage.

0600 – Off watch. Garry sings "Oh, what a beautiful morning" from the Rodgers and Hammerstein 1943 musical *Oklahoma*. At this God-forsaken hour of the morning, it is enough to drive us all into *mourning*.

1400 – On watch. Wind SW (225 deg.), S-20–25 knots, boat C-70 degrees, S-8.5 knots, surging regularly to 9.5 knots. We have set a full main, a staysail, and 90 percent of the genoa, on a broad reach to starboard.

This is an absolutely ideal day with perfect wind conditions for ocean sailing. *Diva* drives full speed ahead through foaming ocean swells that tumble toward her stern deck. As the waves lift her stern, she drops her bow and plunges forward, down the face of the wave in a thunderous rush of foam.

The seas build up dramatically to 12–15 feet, and white caps smother the sea from horizon to horizon. John and I compete avidly to achieve the highest burst of boat speed while surfing down the waves. His top mark is 9.7 knots, while during my trick at the wheel we watch the speed indicator climb through 9.8 to 9.9 to 10.0 up to 10.1 knots. Not once, but twice. When I generously congratulate John, tactfully pointing out the difference between our scores. He responds with a traditional Rhode Island greeting.

1700 – Garry calculates that from 0700 to 1700 hours today, we have sailed 80 miles, a distance that correlates with our speed indicator. We are reassured to know our instrumentation is accurate.

1800 – Off watch. Several bottlenose dolphins cavort alongside *Diva*, rushing and jumping close aboard and leaping under our bow. I try to videotape them, but it proves very difficult to catch their sudden appearances since I cannot anticipate their movements underwater.

Today, as I clamber about the decks and the cabin, I suffer from an extra measure of soreness in my back caused by last night's fall.

1900 – Herb's Weather Service predicts SW winds rising to 25–30 knots tonight. He projects that tomorrow we should pass through a front and pick up northwesterly winds. Thereafter, southwesterlies should prevail, although somewhat lighter than present.

I am particularly tired after my tricks at the helm this afternoon, and probably from my increased back pain. I am very lucky and very grateful, though, to have escaped serious injury.

Wednesday, 7 July 2004 – North Atlantic Ocean 13th Day

Noon Report:
    Position: N-44 degrees 54 minutes, W-33 degrees 27 minutes.
    Barometer: 1025
    Distance: Last 24 hours 194 miles (average speed of 8.1 knots!)
        Total to date: 1,634 miles
        DTG: 1,029 miles
    Wind: SW (225 deg.), S-25–30 knots
    Sky: Variable, overcast with rain and partially clearing
    Sea: SW, 10–12 feet, building to 15 feet
    Current: none
    Boat: C-75 degrees, S-8.5 knots
    S/trim: Broad reach on starboard tack
    Temp: —
    Attire: Sweatshirt, shorts, FWG

0001 – On watch. Wind SW (225 deg.), S-15 knots. The sea is somewhat sloppy and the wave height has fallen considerably to only 4–7 feet. Boat C-73 degrees, S-7.0 knots. Steering requires particular vigilance because the confused seas can suddenly push our heading to leeward into the danger zone, the angle to the wind at which we run the risk of a flying jibe. John and I alternate tricks at the helm every 30 minutes.

It is pronouncedly colder and damper this evening, so I am wearing a sweatshirt and a sweater under my FWG.

0230 – In order to escape the cold, moist ocean air at night, I spend a comfortable rest period under the dodger that shelters the cockpit companionway.

When I stand up to take over the helm, I look forward over the bow and discover a steamer's bright navigation lights at a distance of about two miles, although not yet *close aboard*. She shows a bright red running light in addition to her masthead and range lights. I instantly realize that we are both headed across each other's bows. In short, we are on a collision course with a seagoing citadel of steel, and our closing rate is 27 knots (30 mph)—a combination of her estimated speed of 20 knots plus ours of 7 knots. At our closing rate and at this angle on each other's bows, the distance separating us will disappear at the rate of one mile every three minutes. Thus, we have about 5–7 minutes in which to avoid being run over by a giant steel steamer. (Illustration 39)

38. What I Saw off our Starboard Bow (ER)

Under these circumstances, it is instantly obvious to me that we should not attempt to cross the steamer's bow, so I immediately change course by heading up to starboard in order to pass her port-to-port, which is in accordance with the International Rules of the Road. Once safely past her, I resume our course, passing under her stern. (Illustration 40)

Although we are in no immediate danger and we would have discovered the ship soon enough under any circumstances, in retrospect, I realize that it is fortunate that I stood up when I did. John explains to me that the dodger partially blocks his view when he is at the helm, and its forward windows are too fogged over to see the bow.

At sea, one can never be too vigilant or too careful. Doubtless, one also needs luck. Yesterday evening, I suffered a fall but escaped serious injury, while this evening, I avoided a potentially fatal collision. I am thankful for my Officer of the Deck (OOD) experience in the Navy, which allows me instantly to recognize virtually any ship-handling dangers.

Would the steamer have avoided us if they had chanced to see us? Consider the following widely held view:

Question: What do merchant seamen call a sailboat?
Answer: Something that "goes bump in the night."

0300 – Off watch. DTG is 1,092 miles to Fastnet Rock. Everyone is watching our ship's odometer very intently now. We all want to arrive by July 14th, although presently the 15th seems more attainable.

1000 – On watch. The wind is SW (225 deg.), S-25 knots, gusting to 30 knots, boat C-75 degrees, S-8.5 knots, surging to 9.5 knots. At first the seas are 10–12 feet, then 12 feet, building to 15 feet.

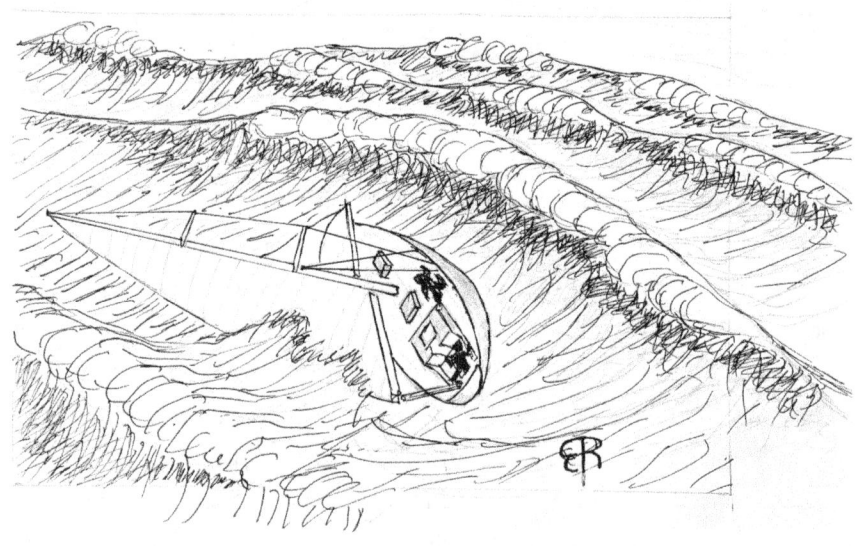

39. Collision-at-Sea Avoidance Maneuver (ER)

I have the first trick on the helm and soon set the speed standard for the watch by surging to 10.6 knots on two occasions. I enjoy owning our high-speed territory, and I am becoming known as the ship's speed-addicted helmsman. After all, there seems little sense in hanging needlessly about the middle of the Atlantic Ocean. In fact, I find it entirely appropriate that I should achieve these records aboard a neuro-*surge*-eon's boat.

John achieves two respectable surges to 10.3 knots but our speedometer readout falters and he sinks below my level. When I congratulate him, he gives me a traditional Rhode Island greeting. I find out that Rob claims our speed record with a surge of 11.0 knots. Any witnesses to this? None comes forward, but since Rob's integrity is unassailable, we accept it as fact. Now I understand how John feels, and with great effort I manage to refrain from using his Rhode Island salutation.

For the past day and night and part of today, we have driven *Diva* relentlessly before strong southwesterly winds and down frothing, tumbling seas. This is a somewhat risky practice that requires masterful, experienced helmsmanship—for which we are all well qualified.

As a result of this demanding situation, we temporarily suspend the services of Otto-the-pilot and take the helm manually to avoid the sickening disaster that lurks in the dreaded, uncontrolled *flying jibe,* which could cause serious damage to our rigging at these wind velocities. The list of potential destruction includes tearing the mainsail, breaking the boom by dipping it into the ocean, breaking our gooseneck, and even dismasting the boat as a result of her broaching and submerging a substantial portion of her mast.

In order to maximize our speed, we must crowd on as much sail as we can carry, and thereby run the risk of a flying jibe. Fortunately, all of *Diva's* crew know just how close to approach the *downwind disaster zone* without incurring its destructive wrath.

The theory of steering downwind under these conditions is clear, but executing it well requires a perceptual sensitivity that can be acquired only from many years of experience at the helm. In short, on any selected course, the sails are set, or trimmed, to produce the maximum power and boat speed. As a result, a boat slows down if waves cause it to veer from its optimum course for which the sails have been trimmed. To maintain the desired course in order to correct this problem, the helmsman steers the boat by swinging the rudder to either side. Each required swing of the rudder, however, causes underwater turbulence that slows the boat.

Thus, since the waves' effects cannot be avoided, the rudder's action must be reduced to the minimum amount needed to maintain the proper course. This is accomplished by anticipating the sea's deflection of the boat's course and by applying just enough rudder angle to forestall it, or *nip it in the bud.* In short, the helmsman or helmswoman is constantly applying anticipatory rudder movements according to the feel of the boat.

This steering practice is beyond the Otto's capability, since the electronic system applies purely reactive rudder adjustments whenever its gyroscopic compass senses a deviation from the prescribed course. Thus, under demanding sea conditions, Otto always runs the risk of applying too little rudder too late to avoid disaster.

1200 – Our noon position is N-44 degrees 54 min, W-33 degrees 27 minutes. Over the last 24 hours we have run 194 miles at the average speed of 8.1 knots. Congratulations to the intrepid helmsmen, to *Diva,* and to the wind gods.

1400 – Off watch.

1525 – We pass the 1,000 miles-to-go mark, and our DTG is now 999 miles, the equivalent of only one-and-a-half Bermuda Races. If we can average 6.0 knots for a daily run of 144 miles, we will need 6.5 more days, resulting in an ETA at Fastnet of Wednesday, July 14th. More conservatively calculated with a boat speed of 5.5 knots, I project our ETA in Kinsale at late Wednesday to early Thursday. John bakes a Thousand-Mile layer cake to honor our Thousand Mile Follies, or as the French say, "mille feuilles."

2100 – On watch. The sailing conditions are absolutely miserable. There is very little wind and it is raining copiously—however, my *sleeve stoppers* work perfectly under these challenging conditions. Wind is

WSW (255 deg.), S-5–8 knots, boat C-75 degrees, S-5.5 knots. We are running dead before the wind, anticipating a wind shift to the NW and a strengthening to 10–15 knots.

2250 - A large cargo ship suddenly looms out of the rain off our starboard bow, then passes aft down our starboard side at 2300 hours, barely 10 minutes after its initial sighting. Low visibility can be dangerous, especially in shipping channels.

2400 – Off watch.

Thursday, 8 July 2004 – North Atlantic Ocean 14th Day

Noon Report:
    Position: N-46 degrees 02 minutes, W-30 degrees 10 minutes.
    Barometer: 1026
    Distance: Last 24 hours 155 miles
       Total to date: 1,786 miles
       DTG: 1,874 miles
    Wind: NW (315-deg.), S-7 knots
    Sky: Overcast with rain with occasional fog
    Sea: NW, 3 feet
    Current: 0.5 – 1.0 favorable
    Boat: C-75-degrees, S-4.0 knots
    S/trim: Reach on port tack
    Temp: —
    Attire: —

0600 – On watch. Wind is NW (315 deg.), S-7 knots, boat C-75, S-4.0 knots.

0800 – We decide to pump our remaining fuel oil reserve from the drums lashed on the fantail, the stern deck, into the main tank in the bilge under the starboard settee. This opens Pandora's Box of troubles.

After our last transfer, we coiled up the fuel hoses and placed them in double plastic bags, where the residual oil in the hoses has leaked out into the bags, coating the tubing with a greasy film of diesel oil. As soon as I open them and remove the hoses, the fuel oil spatters all over the cockpit. What an unholy mess. I manage to keep it from my FWG, but it coats my shoes and turns the cockpit and the surrounding deck into a large, obstacle-strewn skating rink, where maintaining one's balance and moving about are almost impossible.

Using a hand-squeezed pump, Garry and I require about an hour to transfer the fuel, and then the cleanup begins. Rob does an impressively thorough and efficient job of this with a humble pail of hot, soapy water. This is typical of his many quiet contributions to our common welfare.

As a precaution, I suggest we rope off the fantail, using yellow police warning tape. Garry comments that this measure is unnecessary because this area has already been declared a *no-fly zone*, as a result of his policy of not allowing crew members to relieve their urinary waste from the railing on the stern. Hence, no *flies*.

0930 – The fog closes in periodically, reducing our visibility to about half a kilometer, or a quarter of a mile. When the sky lightens unexpectedly, I remark to Neil, our resident Scotsman, that since we are approaching Scottish waters, certainly this must be a sign of the Scottish Enlightenment. Neil beams with justifiable pride, further brightening our day.

1000 – Off watch, just in time to bake a loaf of bread for the first time in my life. If I do it well, I have been promised a CID, or Culinary Institute of *Diva* award. No doubt the first one was awarded to *el Cid*, perhaps for one of his half-baked schemes.

1040 – I receive permission to take a shower. All my shipboard wishes have been fulfilled: personal cleanliness, freshly baked bread, a warm, dry cabin, the hearty camaraderie of one's fellow shipmates, and an opportunity to write a good book—this one. In the background, we enjoy Scarlatti's music. No doubt about it: everything is absolutely *Diva*-ine, even without any wine.

1800 – On watch. Wind is NW (35 deg.), S-7 knots, boat C-75 degrees, S-6.5 knots with the engine running at 1,600 RPM. The sky is overcast and the temperature is plunging sharply.

1830 – Herbert's Weather Service forecasts the wind becoming more westerly with increasing strength, probably by tomorrow. Thereafter, for the next two days, it will veer SW with a strength of 20–30 knots. I ardently hope he is correct. In view of his wind prediction, it makes sense to use our engine now, even though we have fuel for only 300 miles and a DTG of 800 miles. Thus, if we are fully becalmed (as we were in the Bermuda Race), we will be unable to power across a 500-mile gap for lack of sufficient fuel.

1900 – John serves a distinguished dinner of "beef burg-onion" (sic), or some similar fancy French name, followed by fresh apple pie. A glass of well-tempered red wine, such as a Pinot Noir, or a Nuits de St. George, or a St. Emilion would be the perfect accompaniment. Without it, the dinner casts threatening shadows of a *noir nuit*. The lack of a good dinner wine has become our *bete noir*. Maybe Garry simply does not like the French, or perhaps just their musicians. From his musical perspective, do they do *violins* to their instruments by playing them backward?

2050 – Otto-the-pilot suddenly starts flashing a warning message: "power overload," accompanied by an alarm sounding like a British police car. Fortunately, the remaining autopilot functions (other than those that require direct steering control) seem unaffected by this internal electronic altercation.

2100 – Off watch until 0300 hours. I estimate our DTG to Fastnet at 820 miles, plus the distance to Kinsale of 50 miles, for a total of 870 miles remaining. If the winds pick up as predicted, we should be able to average 6 knots for an average daily run of 150 miles, enabling us to arrive in six days, noon-to-noon. Thus, my recalculated ETA is Wednesday, July 14th at 1200 to 1800 hrs. This would be *perfect* (see last day's log entries).

Friday, 9 July 2004 –

North Atlantic Ocean 15th Day

Noon Report:
    Position: N-47 degrees 9 minutes, W-27 degrees 14 minutes.
    Barometer: —
    Distance: Last 24 hours 139 miles
       Total to date: 1,921 miles
       DTG: 735 miles
    Wind: NW (315 deg.), S-8–10 knots
    Sky: Overcast scattered rain, some passing close aboard
    Sea: NW, gentle swells of 2 feet
    Current: 0.5 knots favorable
    Boat: C-75 degrees, S-5.8 knots
    S/trim: Reach on port tack
    Temp: 65 degrees
    Attire: —

0300 – On watch. It is comfortably cool and, thankfully, dry on deck. The wind is NW (315 deg.), S-5–10 knots, boat C-75, S-6.0 knots, powering at 1,700 RPM, with full main and genoa. The ocean is calm with swells from NW, 1–2 feet. We can now make our way about below decks without being thrown around violently by the boat's erratic motion.

We turn on the forced hot air cabin heater, a marvel of the modern sailing age. The temperature below rises quickly to a cozy 73 degrees, while topside it is 63 degrees. Basic comforts make *Diva* a small refuge of heat and life in a cold, gray ocean.

As we work our way northward, we put on full foul weather gear (FWG) every time we go on deck, since we cannot afford to get any of our clothing wet. If it becomes soaked, we will simply freeze.

FWG is made of a coated waterproof skin with an inner layer of insulation material. It consists of high-cut pants in the style of overalls that reach all the way up the top of one's chest and are supported by suspenders. A long jacket is worn over this. All openings have a water trap configuration consisting of heavy-duty zippers on the inside and overlapping Velcro-fastened flaps on the outside. Boots are made of solid rubber and reach halfway up one's calves. The pants are drawn down over the boot tops, and then a waterproof sleeve, attached to the top of the boots, is pulled up over the pants. The seal is then tightened with a drawstring at the top. Inside the boots, I wear athletic socks for warmth. The wrist openings are sealed by Velcro wrist straps. There is an optional hood folded into the back of the collar, as well as a *sou'wester,* a hat that resembles Ponce de Leon's soldiers' helmets with large, protective side flaps that cover my neck. My FWG is a golden yellow for rescue visibility; other available colors include fire engine red. In this decade, FWG has been improved to the point where it begins to resemble an astronaut's spacesuit, seemingly appropriate for use onboard *Diva,* our *terrestrial spaceship.*

Before going on deck to stand my watch, I have to pull on this entire outfit while huge, invisible hands hurl and bounce me about like a basketball in the pitching and heaving cabin. This is why I require twenty minutes to put on my FWG before going on watch.

0600 – Off watch. DTG is 767 miles. I am looking forward to a sound rest with Niko N., AKA Nikon F-4, with whom I have shared my bunk the entire voyage. My beautiful companion has unexcelled capabilities and unsurpassed seductive features that really make us *click* together—she in her camera bag and I in my sleeping bag. I must seek the skipper's advice on how to broach this delicate *affaire de Niko N.* to Nancy.

1200 – New watch assignments:

Transatlantic-4
- A Neil & Ernst
- B Garry & John
- C Rob & Howard

1500 – I cannot believe that I did it. I actually volunteered to bake a loaf of bread, after all my earlier culinary failures. This issue has now become a matter of honor and pride, a rematch between incomplete cooking instructions and my instincts for orderly processing. The oven gives forth early scents of victory, but whose? If I succeed this time, I must take special precautions to ensure that Nancy never learns of my newly acquired culinary skill—otherwise, her cooking demands will rise with the bread.

40. Ernst's Well-Bread Loaf (RL)

1610 – Victory. My loaf of bread turns out to be perfect. It is a true *Rothe* (Rota) *Brot*. "Ist es besser, ein Rotes Brot oder eine Rote Braut zu haben?" Well, that really depends a great deal on the circumstances... and one's taste.

I have lost my fear of the galley. Is this the first step to becoming a galley slave? Am I following a cosmically ordained path of return to my unrecognized Roman or Greek past?

1630 – I have just been asked to prepare dinner after spending the greater part of the afternoon in the galley. I sense that I am increasingly in danger of becoming a galley slave.

1800 – DTG is 699 miles to Fastnet. I am officially on watch, but actually below, preparing dinner. Garry has declared my bread to be, "the best ever made aboard *Diva*." I am surprised and deeply honored. Now, on to the CID (see entry Thursday, July 8th at 1000 hours).

1930 – On watch, on deck. Wind is NW (315 deg.), S-8–12 knots, boat C-77 degrees, S-6.0 knots. The sea is calm with a slight swell.

2100 – Off watch. DTG 677 miles.

Saturday, 10 July 2004 –

North Atlantic Ocean 16th Day

Noon Report:
    Position: N-48 degrees 9 minutes, W-23 degrees 49 minutes.
    Barometer: 1028
    Distance: Last 24 hours 150 miles
       Total to date: 2,069 miles
       DTG: 585/627 miles
    Wind: NNW (335 deg.), S-12 knots
    Sky: Overcast
    Sea: Calm with waves of 1–2 feet
    Current: neutral
    Boat: C-75 degrees, S-6.7 knots
    S/trim: Close each on port tack
    Temp: 65 degrees
    Attire: —

0300 – On watch with Neil. Wind NW (315 deg.), S-8–10 knots, boat C-77 degrees, S-6.5 knots. The wind seems to be picking up. We are on a broad reach on the port tack. It is overcast with occasional light rain showers. There is a band of dark clouds ahead that may portend weather changes—and wind changes?

0445 – Now we have our answer. We are hit by several strong gusts and, within five minutes, the wind shifts from NW (315 deg.) to N (000 deg.) and strengthens considerably to 12–15 knots, putting us on a close reach to port. We trim the main and genoa, which we furl down to 30 percent out. As a result, we are riding comfortably and doing 6.7 knots.

0600 – Off watch. DTG is 620 miles plus 50 miles from Fastnet to Kinsale. If we can maintain 6 knots, we will do 150 miles per day, giving us an ETA in Kinsale of Wednesday evening. How will I photograph our arrival at night?

As we approach our landfall, it seems appropriate to reflect upon life at sea. I think that its greatest impact is its power to strip away all of life's superficiality and pretense, such as office politics, clothing styles, addresses, club memberships, evening news nonsense, politicians' unfulfilled promises, and even socially competitive suburbanites' bragging about some trivial success at the country club. The sea reduces life to its most elemental terms: survival and safety, combined with reasonable progress toward one's goal. These truths become quickly self-evident to anyone on the ocean. You cannot brag about how well you have set a sail when the wind has just torn it off the mast, nor can you comfort yourself by maintaining the self-delusion that it is still affixed to the rigging. You and everyone else can clearly see that the sail has disappeared overboard.

So, perhaps going to sea—or participating in some equally challenging or dangerous activity in nature—is a healthy catharsis that forces us to sort out our values in life and to see more clearly what is true and important, and what is not.

0900 – Garry serves a delicious and fortifying pancake breakfast, for which we are all very grateful.

0915 – DTG is exactly 600 miles.

1215 – In spite of my being in possession of most of my faculties, or so I believe, I agree to bake another loaf of bread. After baking my preparation for some 50 minutes, I open the oven to discover a comatose mass of hardened mush in the bottom of the pan.

I must confess that, although as a baker I am *crustfallen*, I am not otherwise *crestfallen*, having made no claims to any ancestral rights to knighthood, aristocracy, and so forth. Garry and I engage in a lengthy disputative discussion of the relative importance of these terms to bakers and to genealogists. In my opinion, my position would be most difficult for a baker who is descended from a long line of distinguished bakers, rendering him or her both *crust* and *crest* fallen.

Since I am convinced that the oven deliberately sabotaged my efforts, tomorrow we will have a *rematch*—as they say in the oven lighting business.

1400 – On watch. The wind is NNW (330 deg.), S-12 knots, boat C-75 degrees, S-7.3 knots. It is overcast and cold, the temperatures being 71 degrees outside, 71 degrees in the main cabin, and 65 degrees in the forward cabin where I sleep. Attire is sweatshirt, medium sweater, and FWG.

1525 – A ship's superstructure appears on the horizon at about 10 degrees off our port bow. By 1600 hours, she has pulled alongside us on a reciprocal course at a distance of two miles. With an estimated speed of 20–25 knots, plus our 6 knots, the total closing speed is 25–30 knots, equal to one mile every two minutes, or half a mile per minute. On this basis, I calculate our surface visibility at 12–15 miles under clear conditions.

The vessel turns out to be a fully loaded, black-hulled Maersk containership from Denmark.

2330 – The price of safety is eternal vigilance. As I am dozing on the settee in the main cabin, resting before going on watch at midnight, I am vaguely aware of some commotion aft in the galley area. Apparently, we have sprung a leak, and that is definitely a life-threatening matter in the middle of the Atlantic.

Suddenly, our automatic bilge pump starts running for unknown reasons, turning on repeatedly when the bilge should be dry. We immediately conclude water must be entering *Diva's* hull somewhere. Where? We have posted a "through-the-hull" fittings plan, a ship's diagram that shows nineteen valve locations through which water can enter the hull. Since any one of them can rupture, our immediate concern is to find out which one has done so. In hulls with longitudinally segmented bilges, the usual search procedure is to lift up the cabin floorboards, working both forward and aft from the pump's location at the deepest point in the bilge. Since the bottom of the boat slopes upward toward the bow and the stern, and since water flows downhill, one follows the bilge sections successively until finding a dry one. The leak is located one compartment adjacent to that one.

After diligent searching, we find the problem. Our water maker, located aft under the cockpit, has sprung a leak in its output tube and is pouring fresh water into the bilge. It sounds ridiculous that we are literally drowning in our own drinking water. Garry tightens a fitting and we remain safely afloat again. On the ocean, constant vigilance is the price of survival.

Sunday, 11 July 2004 –

North Atlantic Ocean 17th Day

Noon Report:
    Position: N-49 degrees 2 minutes, W-20 degrees 40 minutes.
    Barometer: —
    Distance: Last 24 hours* 137 miles
        *(really 22 hours, for two time zone shifts)
        Total to date: 2,203 miles
        DTG (F): 448 miles
        DTG (K): 490 miles
    Wind: SW (225 deg.), S-10 knots
    Sky: Overcast, scattered low cumulus
    Sea: SW, smooth
    Current: 0.4 knots favorable
    Boat: C-75 degrees, S-6.4 knots
    S/trim: Close reach on starboard tack
    Temp: 59 degrees
    Attire: —

0001 – On watch. Wind is NNW (335 deg.), S-5 knots, boat C-75 degrees, speed 5.5 knots, motoring at 1,500 rpm. It is overcast, but the visibility is good. Quite cold at 52 degrees.

The ocean's phosphorescence at these northern latitudes is exceptional. Our bow waves light up like diagonal cloud lines in the water, while the wake glows like a submerged comet beneath the sea's surface. Farther in the distance, breaking wave tops suddenly flash as erupting bonfires in the night.

0115 – A ship appears in the distance to port, apparently on a reciprocal course, but it is too distant to see its running lights. Its multitude of deck lights are characteristic of a passenger liner.

0220 – The wind collapses entirely upon itself, plunging us into a dead calm. The ocean's surface now shines as a mirror. We turn on the engine. Since all the sails are backing from our forward motion, we furl the genoa and trim the main amidships, increasing power to 1,700 rpm and our speed to 5.8 knots.

0300 – Off watch. DTG is 484 miles.

0830 – 1030 – We set the ship's clock ahead two hours to conform to Ireland's time zone. Therefore, 0830 becomes 1030. As a result, today's noon-to-noon run will be a short one, only 22 hours. This updated navigational fix has been named the "new noon."

Unexpectedly, this morning, the spring for the chime on the ship's clock breaks. Neil proposes that the crew give Garry a new clock with the engraving, "Diva – Transatlantic 2004." (We eventually do, thanks to Rob's personal efforts.)

It is now raining slightly, and the wind freshens to 15 knots.

1400 – Off watch. Garry serves a hearty brunch of corned beef hash with fried eggs and freshly baked blueberry muffins. This meal reminds me of Napoleon's observation that "an army moves on its stomach." Well, so do we.

1640 – I shave and put on a heavyweight blue and red striped rugby shirt for the last leg of our journey.

1805 – I remove my latest culinary creation from the oven. It looks better than the last, but is still a bit disappointing. Its shape seems somewhat flat to me, but hopefully it does not taste flat.

1815 – DTG is exactly 400 miles. We are making 7.7 knots with a 0.7 knot current in our favor. The wind is SSW (205 deg.), S-15–18 knots and freshening. We have averaged 9.2 knots from 1200 to 1800 hours. It seems that the old horse is really racing for the barn.

2100 – On watch. Wind is SSW (200 deg.), S-35 knots with powerful gusts to 40 knots! The boat is on C-80 degrees, S-8.0, on the starboard tack.

As the wind builds rapidly from 25–30 knots to 35–40 knots, the wind attacks our rigging like an infuriated wildcat, howling ferociously in the storm-filled night. We shorten sail as quickly as possible to prevent damage by putting two reefs in the main, furling the genoa completely, and setting the forestaysail. This operation takes Garry and Neil forty minutes of hard work, while I steer. In the middle of it all, we are drenched by flying, driving rain. My glasses fog over so I can no longer see the compass rose. I glimpse our heading only intermittently, while the sea becomes extremely confusing and unpredictable, pushing us off course as much as 20–30 degrees to either side. Through it all, however, *Diva* rides comfortably, under control, on a broad reach to starboard. Regrettably, our prudent sail shortening causes our speed to drop from 8 knots to 6–7 knots, a sacrifice required to achieve our principal goals of survival and steady progress toward our destination.

The North Atlantic is filled with bright patches of phosphorescent light from luminous plankton caught in the breakers' foaming crests. The light patterns resemble fleeting ghosts as they rush toward us in the dark and appear to reach out to grab us as they splash aboard.

2145 – I turn on our radar as a safety measure in the reduced visibility. I place it on standby and activate it every 30 minutes to ensure that we are not surprised by an approaching steamer ahead.

2300 – The wind is starting to slacken to 20 knots with occasional stronger puffs.

2400 – Off watch. DTG is 350 miles.

Monday, 12 July 2004 – North Atlantic Ocean 18th Day

Noon Report:
   Position: N-50 degrees 1 minute, W-16 degrees 37 minutes.
   Barometer: 1024
   Distance: Last 24 hours 168 miles
     Total to date: 2,368 miles
     DTG (F): 280 miles
     DTG (K): 322 miles
   Wind: W (270 deg.), S-12 knots
   Sky: Overcast with intermittent fog
   Sea: W, swells 3–5 feet
   Current: Negligible, 0.2 knots against
   Boat: C-70 degrees, S-7.1 knots
   S/trim: Downwind, port tack, winged out
   Temp: —
   Attire: —

0600 – On watch. Wind WSW (250 deg.), S-5 knots, boat C-80 degrees, S-5.8 knots, powering at 1,700 rpm. We are sailing dead downwind on starboard tack with full main and the genoa furled to prevent backwinding.

0730 – We jibe to port, dead downwind, and unfurl the genoa to 70 percent out to prevent slatting. Boat C-70 degrees S-5.5 knots. Periodically, the fog closes in, reducing our visibility to 200 meters.

0900 – Everyone off watch now comes on deck and studies our sail trim, offering a multitude of unsolicited suggestions for improvement. As if in response to their nagging, the wind picks up from 7 knots to 10–12 knots. The wing watch wings out the genoa on the spinnaker pole to port, and *Diva's* speed promptly ratchets up to 6.2 knots.

Thus, they turn out to be right for the wrong reasons. How often do people attribute their success to their own abilities and intelligence rather than to fortune's favor? Not in this case, but sometimes I wonder.

1000 – The proof is in the boat's speed. DTG 290 miles, and we are now off watch.

Technology is making the North Atlantic more accessible to all sailors who are qualified at boat handling but not proficient navigators. In my opinion, the satellite-based Global Positioning System (GPS) offers unprecedented navigational accuracy, reliability, and above all, ease of use.

In 1960 aboard Watson's *Palawan-2,* we used celestial navigation. It is an arcane, difficult art that only relatively few people can practice competently, but its mastery was absolutely indispensable for sailing beyond the sight of land. Its faults make it unreliable (because it requires visibility to shoot the stars and moon), inaccurate (because a boat's motion can introduce errors into one's celestial angular measurements), and tedious (because it demands considerable proficiency in making complex calculations and chart plots).

Since this skill was required aboard every boat crossing the sea, and since there were few people proficient in this practice, only relatively few boats had the opportunity and the means to cross the Atlantic. Thus, the lack of skill in celestial navigation created a barrier to transatlantic sailing.

Now, the availability of GPS has opened the doors of the North Atlantic to almost everyone due to it making accurate, offshore navigation available to any seasonably intelligent person, irrespective of their level of sailing expertise. In theory, even cross-country campers, bicyclists, and bird watchers could board a boat and set off across an ocean.

In this manner, the true barrier to making a transatlantic passage has now become one's sailing skills and experience. In my opinion, accomplished day sailors and overnight racers with at least a decade of experience stand qualified to make the transition to deep-water voyaging. I emphatically recommend, however, that they do it first as a crewmember on a boat skippered by a proven passage maker. Attention should also be paid to the ruggedness of a boat's construction and rigging.

The most important attitudinal adjustment required for deep-water sailing is to reverse strongly entrenched practices used in around-the-buoy racing. Local racing is intensely focused on short-term boat speed gains, while deep-water sailing is primarily a matter of long-term survival and the achievement of maximum safe speed that does not jeopardize the boat's integrity or risk injury to the crew. The hard truth of the matter is that you are always *on your own* out here, with no immediate assistance available. No one is here to save you from your own folly, mistakes, errors of judgement, inadequate planning, or faulty equipment.

A deep-ocean venture requires thorough organization, detailed preparation, a balanced appraisal of crew members' strengths and weaknesses, an accurate evaluation of the equipment's suitability, and thorough emergency planning. My strongest recommendation is not to cut corners or accept inadequate measures that are considered "good enough." They will surely return to haunt you when you least expect it, and at the least convenient time. It is possible to fool oneself and others for a while, but it is never possible to fool the ocean.

1800 – On watch. Wind has veered to WNW (305 deg.), S-15 knots, boat C-80 degrees, S-7.2 knots. We are running dead before the wind with the pole out to port, wing-on-wing.

2020 – We take the pole down and jibe the genoa to port. The weather is overcast with large swells radiating outward from the center of an intense storm somewhere astern of us.

2100 – Off watch. DTG is now 216 miles, which is slightly more than the distance from New York City to Newport.

At a speed of 6 knots, I calculate we have 36 hours remaining until our arrival at Fastnet on Wednesday, July 14th, at about 0900 hours. To this must be added eight hours for the 47-mile continuation to Kinsale. Thus, depending upon the local tides, we should arrive at Kinsale at 1700 hours. If so, I will be able to photograph our finish.

Tuesday, 13 July 2004 –

North Atlantic Ocean 19th Day

Noon Report:
    Position: N-50 degrees 49 minutes, W-12 degrees 50 minutes.
    Barometer: —
    Distance: Last 24 hours 153 miles
       Total to date: 2,518 miles
       DTG (F): 127 miles
       DTG (K): 169 miles
    Wind: WSW (250 deg.), S-8 knots
    Sky: Overcast with fog, visibility of one kilometer (0.5 miles)
    Sea: W, gentle swells of 4 feet
    Current: Negligible
    Boat: C-080-deg., S-6.4 knots
    S/trim: Downwind, full main and full genoa
    Temp: 58 degrees on deck, 69 degrees below decks
    Attire: —

0300 – On watch. Wind WNW (310 deg.), S-10–15 knots, boat C-80 degrees, S-6.8 knots. The seas are WNW with swells of 4–6 feet, which appear to be from a large storm located in the distance astern. We are so far to the north now that at 0430 hours it becomes light enough to read our wristwatches while on deck.

0600 - Off watch. DTG is 158 miles. Garry has been studying the tidal charts of Ireland's southern coast and approaches. He reports that the current at Fastnet turns favorable (toward the east) tomorrow at 1200 hours. Our ETA at Fastnet is now 0900 hours.

0700 – A fog has closed in, reducing the visibility to under 500 meters (0.25 miles). The wind has died. As soon as we turn on our engine, Garry jumps out of his berth and races to the cockpit companionway. He stares at us disapprovingly from his perch, undoubtedly concerned about our dwindling fuel supplies. Although he probably envisions the possibility of our becoming becalmed and stranded out here, unable to power into port, he is too diplomatic to share his immediate thoughts with us.

Howard, Garry, Neil, and I discuss our options: turn on the engine, turn off the radar, or have a pancake breakfast. We decide I should cook pancakes. Even though it is the first time in my life, the results are excellent regarding taste, texture, color, and even size. I am grateful for the crew's enthusiastic expressions of approval.

0845 – I picked up our first Irish radio station, very faintly and obscured by static. It sounds like a news broadcast.

I sense that land is gradually extending its invisible presence offshore toward us, breaking down the protective isolation of our self-arranged and self-sustained world aboard *Diva*. Today is our last full 24-hour day scheduled at sea. Soon the external world will be "too much upon us." This emotional invasion of our psychic space stirs up impending nostalgia. Arriving at our destination is, indeed, "a time of joy and a time of sorrow," as expressed perfectly in Robert Burns's "Auld Lang Syne."

0915 – DTG is 141 miles. Sitting on the main cabin settee and reflecting upon our voyage, I ask myself, "Are there further tales to tell, or issues to discuss?" Perhaps I have talked and written too much already.

I have heard about the famous English Fastnet Race all my sailing life, and hope fervently that the visibility upon our arrival will be sufficient to permit me to see it—and, just as importantly, to photograph it.

1330 – Garry and Howard serve a hearty, cold weather luncheon of beef and rice soup with grilled cheese sandwiches.

1400 – On watch. Garry and I have a long discussion about the degree to which tastes are learned by cultural exposure (his view) or are intrinsic in one's psychological predisposition (my view). We argue about preferences in food, music, literature, architecture, colors, visual art, sports, and even what constitutes a beautiful woman.

Just as he and I were about to resolve this momentous issue that has confounded the world's great thinkers and philosophers since the origin of civilization, Otto sounds a system overload alarm that requires our immediate attention. I speculate: is Otto trying to express his viewpoint on this matter? Is he overcome by philosophical fear? Or is Otto articulating a subconsciously perceived cosmic warning to Garry and me that we are trespassing into the celestial realm reserved for higher powers?

As a result of Otto's alarm, we will all have to wait until our next transatlantic voyage to learn the answer.

1600 – The wind is dead aft at WSW (255 deg.), S-5–10 knots. Boat's C-75 degrees, S-5.5 knots. We jibe and rig the spinnaker pole to port, with a full genoa set wing-on-wing.

1800 – Off watch. DTG is 132 miles to Kinsale.

1930 - John and I cook the *Captain's Dinner,* which is traditionally served as the evening meal of the last night out. It consists of veal in gravy with mushrooms, beets, and mashed potatoes. Cherries are our dessert.

My toast is short: "Thank you, Garry, for a truly exceptional lifetime experience." To all my fellow crewmembers, I add, "You are the best shipmates one could wish for. I am greatly honored to have shared this special experience with all of you."

2020 – I turn in for a nap before going on the midwatch.

2330 – I wake up and prepare to go on watch.

Wednesday, 14 July 2004 – Bastille Day

Celtic Sea & Southwestern Approaches to Ireland – 20th Day

Noon Report:
　　Position: Piloting along the SW coast of Ireland
　　Barometer: —
　　Distance: See hourly log entries
　　Wind: WNW (285 deg.), S-8 knots, building to 12 knots
　　Sky: Overcast very fog, visibility less than one kilometer (0.5 mi.)
　　Sea: SW, regular swells of 4 feet
　　Current: variable
　　Boat: Base C-80 degrees, S-7.5 knots, various courses and speeds
　　S/trim: Downwind, full main and full genoa, on starboard tack
　　Temp: —
　　Attire: Irish Green

0001 – On watch. Wind WSW (250 deg.), S-5 knots, gusting to 10 knots, boat C-80 degrees, S-6.0 knots. We are running dead downwind with a full main, a furled genoa, and motoring at 1,500 rpm. The sea is calm with two-foot swells from astern. It is overcast and foggy, with visibility varying from 500 meters to 2,000 meters (1.5 miles). Our ETA at Fastnet is now 0800 hours. We should leave it close aboard to port on our way down the southern coast to Kinsale.

0100 – I turn on our radar as a precautionary measure, since we are approaching the United Kingdom's shipping lanes.

0200 – We appear to have wandered into a fishing fleet. There are five radar contacts close aboard within 2–3 kilometers on all sides of us.

Neil terms it "Piccadilly Circus," and since Neil is Scottish, I have a distinct suspicion that this name is not meant as a compliment.

0300 – Off watch. I take a nap with my clothes on, ready to be called on deck for landfall. Dawn brightens the sky already at this hour.

0715 – I awake from nervous anticipation, feeling fully rested after only four hours of sleep. Same weather conditions as before: C-75 degrees, S-6.4 knots, with our genoa furled. We are powering with only the main set. Very heavy fog, visibility 50 meters. DTG 14 miles to Fastnet Rock, and our ETA is 0900 hours.

I can hardly believe that after some 20 days of sailing from Bermuda that landfall is finally at hand. I have heard and read about the famous British Fastnet Race for 50 years, and now I am finally going to see that renowned rock. I am unsettled, however, by the possibility that I might *not* see it because of the fog.

The Fastnet Race is widely respected as one of the world's toughest and most dangerous, because of its predominately severe weather. In 1977, five men were swept overboard and drowned in a savage storm.

Examining the chart of Ireland, our course from Fastnet to Kinsale is filled with a succession of romantic names: Cape Clear, Cullane Bay, Castle Haven, Glandor Bay, Galley Head, Clonakilty Bay, Courtman Sherry Bay, and, perhaps most famous of all, the Old Head of Kinsale, ten miles south of which the Cunard Liner *Lusitania* was torpedoed at 1410 hours on May 7th, 1915 and sank with a loss of 1,198 lives.

For almost two years after the outbreak of the First World War, the United States public did not realize that their own liberty and welfare were somehow connected with England's survival—that is, until they were afflicted with a shared tragedy. Thus, ironically, the *Lusitania's* impact on people's lives was greater in her death than in her life.

0820 – Garry announces that our DTG is 5.0 miles and I volunteer to cook special Fastnet Pancakes to celebrate this historic event.

In honor of our arrival on Bastille Day, I also compose a suitably dignified, commemorative poem to express our ennobling enthusiasm:

C'est la vie,
C'est la mort,
C'est la merde, alors!

0912 – After more than 50 years of anticipation, I am finally rewarded. I see Fastnet Rock abeam to port at a distance of 0.5 kilometers (0.3 miles), with its lighthouse shrouded by a dense fog—known locally as an *Irish mist*. Well, this is one Irish that I would not want to have *missed* (Illustration 42).

41. Fastnet Rock Lighthouse (ER)

0930 – I serve freshly prepared Fastnet-Bastille Day pancakes. To celebrate today's connection with France, I rename Rob "Robs-Pierre" and John Quinn "John Guillo-Quine," in honor of the French dual-purpose machine for slicing bread and removing heads. I wonder: Do they wipe the blade between applications? In either case, this tribute gives all of us fair warning to *sharpen up*.

1000 – On watch. Wind WSW (250 deg.), S-12 knots, boat C-80 degrees, S-7.1 knots. We are running dead downwind under full main and furled genoa, and we are running our engine at 1,700 rpm.

Visibility is 1,200 meters, completely hiding Ireland from our view as we run parallel to its south shore.

1300 – We set our clocks ahead one hour to conform to local Irish time. Since the clocks are reset to 1400 hours, I go off watch immediately but remain on deck.

1450 – Wind piping up nicely to a steady 12 knots and gusting to 15 knots, giving us a speed of 7.5–8.0 knots.

1505 – I take a gloriously refreshing shower, shave, and brush my teeth. I feel properly groomed for going ashore this evening without incurring any danger of disgracing *Diva* or its crew.

1515 – We jibe onto the port tack and head up to a course of 20 degrees to fetch the Old Head of Kinsale, keeping it off our port bow.

1605 – I hear a distant foghorn broad on our port bow. I suspect it is a whistler buoy, although the regularity of its blast indicates it may be a lighthouse, perhaps that of Kinsale. Because the fog limits our visibility to 1.5 kilometers (1 mile), we cannot see the shore yet.

1615 – I confirm our first landfall by sighting the Old Head of Kinsale (OHK), broad on our port bow. I cannot see the bluffs yet, just the white surf breaking against the base of the cliffs. Gradually, like a developing photograph, the land's form becomes visible—first hinting at its outline, and later filling in a solid, recognizable image.

1645 – We pass OHK, leaving it abeam to port, and enter outer Kinsale Bay. I keep a lookout on the bow for buoys marking the location of fishing nets.

1730 – We douse and furl our main and proceed under power into the inner Kinsale Bay and harbor, passing an abandoned, somber, stone fortress to starboard.

1812 – We approach the marina and I cast our bowline over to moor alongside the sloop *Pinnochio*. Our 24-day voyage has now officially ended! Rob's family meets us at the pier and comes aboard to give us a heartfelt welcome. What a wonderful family they are, and how rewarding it is to be welcomed by such fine, warm people in a foreign port.

Garry serves champagne, confirming my suspicion that the *Diva* was not completely dry.

1915 – Except for Rob, who leaves with his family, we all set off for a civilized dinner in town. The ocean's swell is still within my inner ear as I feel the pavement heaving under foot. This "inner motion" causes me to stagger about and stumble from the sidewalk into the street.

2250 – I talk to Whit in Newport on Howard's transatlantic cell phone to wish him a Happy 21st Birthday for tomorrow, July 15th. Nancy is attending a Newport Music Festival concert. Everyone at home is fine. Thank God for that, and for my safe arrival. I plan to call Nancy tomorrow, late afternoon local Newport time, before family and friends head out to celebrate Whit's birthday.

Upon our return to *Diva*, Garry lit a kerosene anchor lantern, a traditional beacon for every sailor's safe return.

The Brown University motto fittingly expresses our gratitude: "In Deo Speramus." In God we hope, and we trust…we certainly do.

APPENDIX - A

Sailing Biographies

1. **Edwin G. (Garry) Fischer**

Our skipper, Garry Fischer, has sailed since the age of seven, when his father purchased a surplus rubber raft carried by aircraft for rescue purposes during the Second World War. Garry's first command at sea hailed from the homeport of Huntington, Long Island. She had a triangular red sail that hoisted on a mast and was handheld at the tack and the clew. Lacking a keel, she excelled at downwind sailing.

Garry's next command was a lapstrake Dyer dinghy, nine feet overall, that he sailed from the Noroton Yacht Club, starting 1948.

In 1969, he moved up to an O'Day Mariner. With a LOA of 19 feet, she had two berths and a head, rendering her fully equipped for regular offshore cruises from her homeport of Marion, Massachusetts, to Newport, with an overnight respite in Cuttyhunk.

In the 1970s, Garry solved his need for more than two bunks by acquiring a Tartan-30, aboard which he cruised often "down east" to Maine and competed in races held during New York Yacht Club cruises.

In the 1980s, he shifted to a Sabre-34, which he used for racing in Narragansett Bay and cruising to Nova Scotia.

Garry started to realize his deep-water sailing goals when he bought an Ocean Cruising (OC) 39 built by Hank Hinckley. He named her *Tempo*. Aboard her, he realized what can only be called "every sailor's dream cruise scenario" over the course of four years in Northern Europe.

During the first year, *Tempo* sailed to Scotland where his cousins live and cruised the Hebrides. The next year, he crossed the Caledonian Canal and sailed across the North Sea to Norway, then through the Gota Canal in Sweden from Goteborg to Stockholm on the shores of the Baltic, where he left his boat for the winter. In the third year, *Tempo* cruised east from Sweden along the Aaland Island chain to Helsinki, doubling back westward across the Baltic to Gotland, proceeded southward to Kalmar, to Denmark, then to Kiel and the Kiel Canal, and finally to Glückstadt on the Elbe River, where *Tempo* was left for the third winter. The fourth year, he headed south along the Friesian Islands, past Rotterdam, and down to the English Channel, calling on

Dover, Bornemouth, Plymouth, and the Scilly Islands before crossing to Kinsale to cruise the south coast of Ireland, where *Tempo* was stored for the winter. She was sailed home the next spring by an Irish friend.

His only other significant sailing, aside from Bermuda Races, was taking *Diva* from Bermuda to Scotland to cruise the Hebrides again with his cousins in 2000, and bringing her back to Newport via Ireland, the Azores, and Bermuda the following year.

2. HOWARD EISENBERG

Howard is a neurosurgeon, residing in Baltimore. He keeps his dark blue Baltic-43, *Midnight Sun,* at a NYYC Harbor Court mooring in Newport. Thus, he is well situated for frequent short cruises to Martha's Vineyard, Nantucket, Block Island, and the nearby New England ports.

He started his sailing career in Sunfishes in Casco, Maine, near Sebago. His boating experience is unusually varied. After graduation from medical school, he worked at New York Hospital where he looked out the windows at the East River, admiring the passing sailboats. Later, when he served in the US Navy, he spent four months at the Great Lakes Naval Base, where he crewed with friends for evening outings on a 50-footer. Thereafter, he started crewing for Garry whenever he came to Newport. When Howard moved to Galveston, a friend lent him a 36-foot sloop in return for paying the operating expenses. Eventually, he bought a Camper Nicholson 35-footer and then a Baltic-38. He participated in several regattas between Houston and Port Aransis, near Corpus Christi. When he moved to Maryland, he sailed his boat from Texas to Baltimore and then traded up to his present Baltic-43.

His racing experience includes a Newport-to-Bermuda race and a Marion-to-Bermuda race with Garry, as well as a Florida-to-Bermuda race, two Newport-to-Bermuda races without Garry, and a Marblehead-to-Halifax race on *Midnight Sun.*

Other offshore sailing adventures include sailing from Rome to Sardinia and Corsica, cruising through the Stockholm archipelago in Sweden, transiting the Inland Sea of Japan, coastal sailing in Italy from

Tuscany to Portofino, and sailing around Oahu, Hawaii, and around Bora Bora.

On the helm, Howard holds a course with relentless, surgical precision heedless of any raging gales or ocean tumult.

3. Rob Leeson

Rob is a Rhode Islander who has traveled considerably for business and pleasure, especially in Europe, East Asia, and Southeast Asia, and presently resides in Narragansett, overlooking the Atlantic.

He cut his teeth at about five, racing and sailing 12-foot Skidoos in the Fishers Island Sound, followed by Bulls Eyes and then H 24's. He soon began to sail Lawley 15's in Saunderstown, RI, where there was a large, active racing program. He also taught sailing for many years to the youth of Fishers Island and Saunderstown.

During the early 1950s, Rob became interested in ocean racing and sailed with his father on his 39-foot Rhodes double-ended cutter *Narwhal*, racing to Bermuda, Halifax, and other local overnight races. Ocean racing, along with cruising on *Narwhal*, continued to interest him, and so did regular participation in numerous ocean races on *Blue Water, Magic Carpet,* and *Viking*. He has participated in seven Newport to Bermuda races, three Marblehead to Halifax races, and three Annapolis to Newport races, as well as races from Cape May to Newport, from Stamford to Vineyard, Monhegan Island, and other local races.

Rob joined CCA in 1966, has served on its Board, and has for the past ten years been active on the Newport-Bermuda Race Committee.

For about 35 years his family owned a 1958 42-foot Alden Nordfarer yawl, *Hope San*, built by Cheoy Lee, which they cruised extensively in New England waters and regularly raced in the Museum of Yachting's Classic Yacht Regatta. He and his wife took great pride in doing their best to keep her in "Bristol fashion."

Other cruising experiences have taken him many times up and down the New England coast, east to Cape Breton Island and Nova Scotia, and south to Maryland, as well as to Greece, Turkey, Yugoslavia, Scotland, Ireland, and most of the Caribbean.

Not owning an ocean cruiser or racer himself these days, Rob spends his time on the water sailing with others—but his fleet still includes a Windsurfer, Laser, Dyer sailing dinghy, a couple of duck boats, and a kayak.

Sailing instruction for his growing family of eight grandchildren is, hopefully, in the future....

Accomplished at getting a boat going in virtually any wind or sea condition, Rob applies his sailing and helmsman experience quietly, allowing the boat's speed to speak for itself.

4. Neil Macaulay

Neil is Garry's cousin by marriage. He presently lives outside Glasgow and holds the important office of *Diva's* Resident Scotsman. Neil was born and raised in Kenya and started sailing at the age of seven with his relatives when he visited them back in the UK.

Neil spent twenty-two years in the British Army, fifteen of which he served both as a fixed-wing pilot of de Havilland Beavers and as a helicopter pilot. He flew mostly in Ireland and in western Canada, and also ventured as far south as Curacao and Aruba.

Sailing has been an enduring passion, and Neil has cruised in the Plymouth area, the Solent, and even in Eastern Asia. Several years ago, he cruised with Garry from Glasgow to Cork, then to the Azores, and from there to Newport, RI.

For our passage, Neil contributes his expertise in weather interpretation and forecasting based on his pilot's background. In addition to his enthusiastic participation in all maneuvers, he brings expertise in brewing the best British *afternoon spot of tea*, which has revived many a weary watch stander. Neil's dry Scottish wit is appreciated by even those who profess not to understand it. Certainly, no one can ignore it.

Neil's hand steadies the kicking helm, no matter how rough the seas become.

5. John C. Quinn

John Quinn's sailing expertise and experience are so vast that they literally speak for themselves.

October, 2003 – Annual "Old Gents" Cruise from Jamestown to Cuttyhunk, Wings Neck, Hadley's Harbor, and the Kickamuit River aboard *Harrier*, Concordia 41.

October, 2001 – Annual "Old Gents Cruise" from Jamestown to Cuttyhunk, Block Island, Shelter Island, Stonington, and Mystic aboard *Harrier*.

October, 2000 – Annual "Old Gents Cruise" from Jamestown to Block Island, Stonington, Connecticut River (Hamburg Cove), back to Stonington, Mystic aboard *Harrier*.

Marion to Bermuda Races
1989 – aboard Cricket
1981 – aboard *Harrier*
1977 – aboard *Harrier*

Newport to Bermuda Races
1980 – aboard *Harrier*
1978 – aboard *Brass Ring*
1976 – aboard *Harrier*
1974 – aboard *Freebooter*
1970 – aboard *Harrier*
1968 – aboard *Harrier*
1966 – aboard *Harrier*
1964 – aboard *Harrier*
1962 – aboard *Harrier*
1958 – aboard *Sea Lion*

Annapolis to Newport Race
1961 – aboard *Harrier*

Marblehead to Halifax Race
1977–1981 – aboard *Harrier*

Other Races
The Storm Trysail Block Island Race
The Whaler's Race from the New Bedford YC

NYYC Cruises – early 1950s – 3 or 4 cruises aboard *Dauntless*

College – Brown University, AB – Class of 1957
1992 – Elected to the ICYRA (College Sailing) Hall of Fame
1956 – Intercollegiate National Championships
1956 – Brown win the Easterns (Owen Trophy)
1956 – Brown won the McMillan Cup (Intercollegiate Big Boat Championship in USNA 44' Luders Yawls)
1954–1955 – on the Timme Angsten Thanksgiving Series in Chicago
1953 – N.E. Freshman Championships (Nickerson Trophy)

Clubs and Associations
1971 & 1972 Conanicut Yacht Club (CYC), RC Chairman, Commodore
1990–2002 New York Yacht Club – Masters Team Racing Program for both the NYYC and against them (for CYC)

Narragansett Bay Yachting Association
1960s–mid 1990s – Cruising Class Chairman, President 1983–4, Chairman of Appeals Committee
New England Yacht Racing Council – President 1983, Secretary/Treasurer 1985–86
NAYRU/USYRU/USSA – Chairman for the Jury for 1977 America's Cup Challengers Eliminations and member of the Jury for the 1980 Challengers Eliminations
Brown University Yacht Club – 1953–7, Commodore in 1957

6. Ernst Rothe

Ernst's sailing career began at the age of nine, when his father purchased a cruising 8-meter in Sweden, named *Schnapps,* which he raced out of the Indian Harbor Yacht Club. Ernst participated regularly in Block Island and Stamford-Vineyard Races for more than a decade. Eventually, this boat was replaced by a Block Island-40, which they sailed for a decade and then a Swan-48, named *Kirsten,* which they kept for some 24 years. Ernst raced actively on board all of them for many years in several Newport-Bermuda races and Annapolis-Newport races.

Half a dozen summers were spent cruising "down east" to Maine, particularly in the region between Camden and Mount Desert Island, including Somes Sound. Summer cruises south of Cape Cod were to Mystic, Nantucket, Edgartown, Block Island, and Newport. Part of each summer included the annual New York Yacht Club cruise, during which Ernst raced in the company of the legendary yachts of the wooden era: *Bolero, Baruna, Nina, Cotton Blossom, Good News, Mustang, Vim* (12-meter), *Revenoc, Gleam* (12-meter), *Windigo, Finisterre*, and *Palawan*.

Ernst also usually spent a portion of his summers in Scandinavia, where the family's racing 6-meter named *Lillian* was used for cruising around Denmark.

Ernst's sailing experience increased significantly when he crewed for several years aboard Thomas J. Watson Jr.'s *Palawan-2*, a 54-foot sloop. He first participated in a cruise around Zealand, Denmark, then onward to Sweden. In the US, races included Stamford-Vinyard, Block Island, Monhegan, NYYC regattas, and Annapolis-to-Newport, culminating in 1960 when he participated in the Newport-to-Bermuda Race and then raced 3,000 miles from Bermuda to Marstrand, Sweden.

Presently, he sails regularly out of Newport on OPBs—other people's boats. Last year, he cruised aboard *Echo*, a 52-foot J-169, from Newport to the Bras d'Or Lake via Nova Scotia.

To quote one of *Diva's* crew members, "Ernst's positive approach and enthusiastic attitude, coupled with his unparalleled seamanship, ensured that the entire crew remained in good spirits at all times, even after three straight days of rain and miserable conditions."

APPENDIX – B

Compass Rose and Glossary

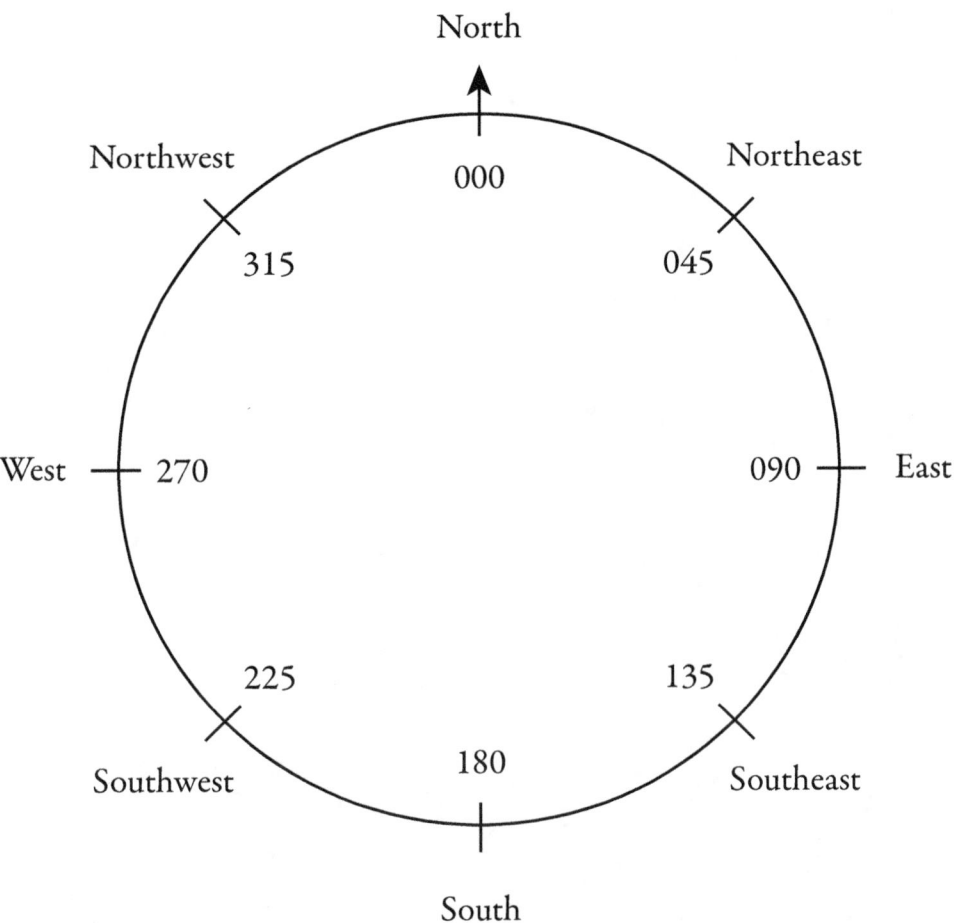

42. Compass Rose (ER)

Glossary of Nautical Terms

This glossary includes primarily nautical terms used in this log, plus related ones used to define the principal terms. It is intended principally to assist the non-sailor and is, by no means, a comprehensive dictionary.

Abeam – "off the beam," or directly off the side or perpendicular to a boat's longitudinal axis

Above – referring to course, to windward of the desired course

Aft – toward the stern, or back of a boat

Athwartships – from side-to-side, across the beam of a boat

Back/backing – to rig a sail in such a manner that it propels a boat backward, or swings the bow away from the wind

Base course – desired course, usually the rhumb line course

Batten – a thin strip of rigid material inserted into a pocket on a sail for the purpose of preventing flutter

Beam - width of a boat

Beat – to sail against the wind by tacking alternately back and forth in a zigzagging manner; see "upwind"

Before the wind – to leeward, or in the direction of the wind

Below – also, "down below," below decks in the cabin

Below – referring to a course, to leeward of the desired course

Boom – horizontal spar on which the mainsail is rigged and simultaneously on the mast

Bow – the front, or forward, part of a boat

Buoy – a floating, anchored navigational mark, often equipped with a signaling device, such as a light, bell, or whistler

Canvas – sails

Class – a type of boat of the same design; also, a group of similar boats in a race

Close hauled – sailing upwind, or against the wind, as close to its reciprocal direction as possible

Cockpit – a sheltered area recessed into the deck with seats, usually located aft

Companionway – a vertical opening, functioning as a "doorway"

Cotter pin – a locking wire to secure fasteners and/or prevent movement of rigging devices, such as turnbuckles

Course – direction steered, usually indicated by a magnetic compass's bearing

Dead astern – directly off the stern; also "dead aft"

Dead downwind – directly before the wind; in the same direction as the wind

Deck – the topmost, horizontal surface of the hull; also, "on deck," as in on the deck or in the cockpit, not below in the cabin

Dodger – a protective folding structure of canvas located at the forward end of the cockpit covering the main hatch

Downwind – to leeward, or in the direction of the wind

Ease – referring to sail trim, to let out, to adjust its angle, sometimes increasing its curvature, for sailing less close hauled or downwind

Ease – referring to lines, to let out, to reduce tension upon

Flying jibe – jibing accompanied by the boom's swinging freely and wildly across the deck due to a lack of restraining lines or "preventers"

Foredeck – portion of the deck forward of the foremost mast

Foresail – a sail rigged forward of the mast which sometimes extends aft of the mast

Forward – toward the bow, or front of the boat

Foul Weather Gear (FWG) – waterproof outer clothing

Furl – to secure, or put away, a sail by gathering, rolling, or folding it up

Gear – personal belongings

Genoa – a foresail, rigged forward of the mast, usually extending aft of it

Gun – a cannon used for signaling by a race committee
Guy – both fore and after, an adjustable line or wire used to position a spar horizontally, such as a spinnaker pole

Halyard – a line for hoisting a sail, usually up a spar
Hatch – an opening, usually horizontal, in the deck
Heel – to incline, or tip, to one side
Helm – used to steer a boat, usually a wheel on a binnacle, or a tiller, usually located in the after part of the cockpit
Helmsman – person at the helm, steering the boat

Jib – a foresail, rigged forward of the mast and not extending aft of it
Jibe – to change course by swinging the stern into the wind so as to bring the wind direction to the other side of the boat

Knot – a unit of speed equal to one nautical mile (6,080 feet) per hour

Latitude – location, north or south, along a meridian
Launch – small motorboat for ferrying people between the shore and vessels anchored out
Leeward – downwind or to leeward, in the direction of the wind
Length – of hull, see LOA
Lifelines – a fence-like structure rigged along the rail, enclosing the deck space to prevent people's falling overboard
Line – a rope used for hoisting a sail (halyard), trimming a sail (sheet), positioning a spar (guy), or securing something
Length-Over-All (LOA) – total length of a boat's hull as measured from stem to stern on deck
Longitude – location, east or west upon a line of latitude
Length-on-the-Water Line (LWL) – length of the hull at the level upon which the boat floats

Main – mainsail, the principal sail, located aft of and attached to the main mast and a boom
Mainmast – the principal, and usually the largest, mast

Mast – vertical spar upon which sails are rigged
Masthead light – navigation light, white, at the top of the mast, usually the mainmast, visible in a 360-degree arc
Mooring – anchor, line, and float, not stowed aboard the vessel using it

Navigation lights – (on *Diva*) masthead, running, and stern lights

Offshore – beyond the sight of land
Over canvassed – carrying or setting too much sail
Overhang – that portion of the bow or stern extending beyond the length of the waterline

Pitching – inclining alternately from stem to stern
Port – left-hand side or direction; also a place of refuge, usually including an anchorage and a settlement
Position – location of vessel, when offshore, stated as latitude and longitude
Pulpit – a fence-like structure located in the bow and in the stern to prevent people's falling overboard

Quarter – a 45-degree arc to either side of the centerline, astern of the vessel

Rail – portion of the hull above the deck line and surrounding the deck; also railing
Reach – to sail with the wind directly from the side, or off the beam
Rigging – the propulsion surfaces of a sailing vessel, including spars, sails and their positioning and control lines including lines for hoisting (halyards) and for trimming (sheets)
Rig – same as rigging; also, a particular arrangement of sails, such as a sloop; also to position something for use, such as rigging a jib; also, to attach a line or sail to something
Rhumb line – shortest distance between two points on a globe
Roll – also rolling; inclining alternately from side to side
Run – to sail downwind, with the wind either dead astern or off either stern quarter

Running light – navigation light, red or green, indicating which side the vessel is showing to the viewer

Running rigging – adjustable control elements of a rig or rigging, such as sheets

Shrouds – stays rigged from the lower part of the mast athwartships to the railing in order to support the mast

Sloop – a sailboat with a single mast

Spar – a rigid, usually tubular, structural part of the rigging, such as a mast, boom, spinnaker pole, etc. that supports the sails

Spinnaker – large racing foresail resembling a balloon or bulbous kite

Spinnaker pole – a horizontal spar on which is rigged a spinnaker

Standing rigging – spars and support elements of a rigging or rig

Starboard – right-hand side or direction

Stays – fixed rigging: wires, or rods, that hold up the mast and sometimes accept the attachment of sails (see forestay)

Steerage – also, steerage way, having motion, usually headway, sufficient for steering control

Stem – the bow portion of the hull

Stern – back, or after, part of a boat

Stern light – navigation light, white, mounted on the stern and visible from an arc of 45 degrees to either side of the stern

Stow – to put in its proper place; to store

Surging – accelerating temporarily to a speed exceeding theoretical hull speed, usually while traveling down a wave

Tack – a boat's orientation relative to the wind, either port or starboard; also, to change course by swinging the bow into the wind so as to bring the wind direction to the other side of the boat; also, the lower forward corner of a sail

Tacking – to tack repeatedly against the wind while travelling to windward in a zigzag course

Tender – an auxiliary craft, such as a launch, for rendering support services to a larger vessel

Topping lift – a line used to support or hoist a spar

Topsides – that portion of the hull above the waterline; also location on deck

Trim – referring to sail trim, to bring in a sail, thereby flattening it or reducing its curvature, in order to sail upwind

Trim – referring to lines, to increase the tension on

Trim – referring to flotation, the degree to which a vessel floats according to its designed water line, which depends upon its buoyancy and loading

Turnbuckles – a double-ended screw-like device attached to and used for adjusting the tension of standing rigging, such as stays, lifelines, etc.

Underway – not secured to land, such as a harbor bottom, shore, or pier

Unfurl – to set or let out a sail; the reverse of furling

Upwind – to windward, or in the direction of the wind; see "beat"

Watch – a designated time period during which selected crew members sail a vessel; a group of crew members forming such a team

Waterline – see "LWL"; see "Trim"

Windward – into the wind or against the direction from which the wind is blowing; the opposite of downwind

Wing-on-wing – sailing with sails, usually the main and the foresail, rigged opposite each other, usually dead downwind

www.ingramcontent.com/pod-product-compliance
Lightning Source LLC
Chambersburg PA
CBHW080457240426
43673CB00005B/216